The Lion's Country

The Lion's Country

C. S. Lewis's Theory of the Real

Charlie W. Starr

The Kent State University Press   Kent, Ohio

© 2022 by The Kent State University Press, Kent, Ohio 44242

All rights reserved

ISBN 978-1-60635-453-7

Manufactured in the United States of America

Cataloging information for this title is available at the Library of Congress.

26 25 24 23 22   5 4 3 2 1

To Bryan and Kathy Rife,

the most real people I know

Contents

Foreword

Diana Pavlac Glyer

Think back to a recent time when you connected with a good friend, maybe over coffee or lunch, a time when you met together to talk and laugh and share. That *real* event really happened. And now, thinking back, you remember specific details: you recall the *truth*, if you will. Tom was wearing a blue shirt. There was a berry pie. The weather was cold.

Add to that memory a few more layers: How did you feel about that meeting? How do you evaluate the importance of it? What insights and possibilities did it hold?

Reality: It happened. *Truth*: An accurate account of that reality. *Interpretation*: How we wrestle to make sense of it. Philosophers delight to consider such definitions and distinctions. C. S. Lewis received a "first" in both classics and philosophy in 1922, and he became a philosophy tutor at University College, Oxford, in 1924. By the end of his first year, though, Lewis questioned his calling. In a letter to his father, he concludes, "I have not the brain and nerves for a life of pure philosophy. A continued search among the abstract roots of things, a perpetual questioning of all that plain men take for granted ... is this the best life for temperaments such as ours?" (*Collected Letters* 1: 648–49). Lewis shifted to the study of literary history and criticism, and he spent the remainder of his career as a teacher of English literature.

Although he changed his academic affiliation, he never abandoned the habits of mind he learned under the tutelage of William Kirkpatrick and throughout the years of his undergraduate education. This is evident throughout his writings, for many of Lewis's most important contributions address life's great questions in philosophical terms. *The Abolition of Man* is one important example. His essay "Myth Became Fact" is another. We find this approach again in *The Problem of Pain, Miracles: A Preliminary Study*, and *Mere Christianity*.

But, as Charlie Starr observes, it doesn't stop there. Both *Till We Have Faces* and *A Grief Observed* can be understood as a reflection on the way that perception shapes our reality. *The Great Divorce* demonstrates that we must be willing to accommodate ourselves to reality (and not the other way around). *Letters to Malcolm* declares that God must, in mercy, shatter our ideas of him in order that we might know reality. Once you go looking for it, you see it everywhere.

Even the most accessible of Lewis's works, *The Chronicles of Narnia*, contains significant insights gained through the lens of philosophical inquiry. Starr points out that *The Silver Chair* is fundamentally a book about knowledge. He writes, "how can we know? How can we be sure? Ultimately what it's asking, though, is what is *real?*" (page 48). And Lewis raises that same question yet again in *The Last Battle* by presenting the dwarves who are sitting in heaven but see only a stable; they're surrounded by brilliant light but see nothing but darkness; they're given a banquet of the finest foods but taste only hay and old vegetables (page 50). Their stubborn presuppositions blind them to what is really real.

What is real? What are the essential distinctions between reality, fact, and truth? Is the immediate more real than the transcendent? Is the visible more real than the invisible? For those who do not naturally gravitate toward these kinds of questions, it all might seem to be merely a matter of picky semantics.

And yet, even if we are not inclined to devote our best attention to the pursuit of philosophical questions, I would argue that we have a lot to gain from those who have. It can do us a world of good to read authors like Charlie Starr in order to have our thinking process clarified, our foggy notions brushed away, and our vague understanding replaced with greater insight and precision. While it is right to celebrate Lewis's creative accomplishment and enjoy his original approach to eternal issues, there are also a number ways he can clear the cobwebs and challenge not only *what* we think, but *how*. That is the beauty of this book. *The Lion's Country* clearly delineates one of Lewis's most important contributions—how he thinks about the essence of reality itself—and then traces this idea through his books, sermons, and essays.

Even more, those of us who love the works of C. S. Lewis have a lot to gain from this thoughtful, extended treatment of how certain key ideas—terms such as fact, reality, myth, transcendence, meaning, beauty, joy, the numinous, and the absolute—function throughout the writing of C. S. Lewis. Lewis is a joy to read and a pleasure to study. But at times, even the most seasoned Lewis scholars head off in the wrong direction because they have used the everyday definition of a word rather than the technical definition that Lewis is employing.

It is Lewis's great friend J. R. R. Tolkien who illuminates the reason this is of such great value to both the fan and the scholar: "The chief purpose of life for any of us," Tolkien says in a letter, "is to increase according to our capacity our knowledge of God by all means we have, and to be moved by it to praise and thanks" (May 20, 1969).

Good philosophy, and good books like this one, counter the insidious poison of bad philosophy. Teach us to practice better habits of mind. Show us how to interact more faithfully with the world God made. And help us to read C. S. Lewis with greater understanding, precision, and pleasure. Even more, pondering the nature of reality has the power to inch us even closer to the One who is not only the Way and the Life but the Truth. And, moved by it, to lift our hearts in praise and thanks.

Preface

There is some irony in my saying this book is for people who have a passion for truth because, ultimately, it's not a book about truth. In fact, like me, you may be surprised to learn that C. S. Lewis, widely known as an apologist and champion of what he called "mere" Christianity, was *not* primarily interested in *Truth*. He was after something more. In his writings (some forty books, hundreds of essays and poems, and thousands of letters), Lewis shows a remarkable ability to stop you in your tracks and change the trajectory of your thoughts, even the way you think, forever. The direction-changing sentence I once encountered is in Lewis's essay, "Myth Became Fact." While talking about the complexities of knowledge and myth, Lewis makes this distinction: "truth is always *about* something, but reality is that *about which* truth is" ("Myth Became Fact" 66). I learned from Lewis that here was an epistemological tool—a tool about the nature of knowing and how it works—a tool that was absent from my education and was absent during the Modernist period in which Lewis wrote. It is simply that there is a distinction between fact (or reality) and truth.

The loss of this distinction can be traced easily enough, beginning with the rise of the concept of the undeniable, individual, utterly knowable *fact*, a concept that emerged slowly but early in the scientific revolution in Christian Europe (see Donald Cowan's *Unbinding Prometheus*). Where the great thinkers of the West had looked to a wholistic understanding of nature, relying on thought models of what they supposed nature to be like, understanding the limits of their pursuit of knowledge, the rise of the idea of the atomistic fact drove thought about truth from a sense of the whole to individual parts, and from a belief in accurate models to a belief in absolute knowledge.[1] Thus, Galileo got himself in trouble with the church, not for any anti-Christian claims in his science, but for believing that the Copernican model of the universe wasn't merely a model but was absolute fact. Then, after the Age of Reason elevated one kind of knowing to supremacy, casting doubt on even the legitimacy of other (say poetic) modes of knowing (despite the Romantics' best attempts to stem the tide), philosophy embraced the increasing influence of science, narrowing the scope of what is epistemologically acceptable even more, so that by the time C. S. Lewis entered college and then became a teacher in philosophy and Medieval and Renaissance literature in the 1920s, logical positivism has risen to claim that the only legitimate knowledge at all is the knowledge of facts—a knowledge that exists without the need for subjective interpretation, a knowledge that is wholly objective, and a knowledge that is utterly inarguable. In other words, by the early twentieth century, the only truth in existence was fact, fact the only truth, and the only distinction that needed to be made in human knowing was that between *fact* and *opinion*.[2]

1. Lewis's friend and fellow Inkling Owen Barfield discusses this idea in *Saving the Appearances*.
2. On the limiting of modes of knowledge in Western thought I recommend Guite's *Faith, Hope and Poetry*.

C. S. Lewis rejected this myopic view of knowledge even before he became a Christian. While his total epistemology is complex, Lewis generally writes of truth as an abstraction (there are some exceptions that we'll get to), a step back from reality (the word *abstract* comes from a Latin word meaning *to separate*). Truth is something going on in our heads (though, for Lewis, not in any postmodern, we-invent-our-own-truth sense). It happens when what we think *about* reality is accurate—when the thoughts in our heads correspond with reality outside our heads, they are true thoughts. If I see a tree and think, "This is a gopher," and I mean that literally without any recourse to imaginative play or poetic device, I am wrong. Sometimes the thoughts in our heads do not correspond with reality. In those instances (excepting poetic purposes), our thoughts are lies or falsehoods, not truths.

My initial point of emphasis is Lewis's understanding that *truth* and *fact* are not synonymous. Science itself, where the distinctions were first blurred (not so much by scientists as by what Lewis would call "scientism"), is ironically the best place to prove that Lewis's distinction is correct. We think of science as a discipline that works with facts. Science doesn't render opinions, science doesn't play with theory, science finds ways to get at the facts. If that were true, however, there would never be a need to write new science books. Science used to teach us that the Grand Canyon was fifty million years old. Now it teaches us that the Grand Canyon is five million years old. That's a pretty big miss. If science dealt solely in fact, it would never have to correct itself. But correcting itself is something science rightly tries to do all the time, sometimes reluctantly but often deliberately and with strict, rigorous testing criteria. What too many people fail to realize or have even been wrongly taught, is that no human being deals with facts alone. Our very thought processes require us to deal not just in fact but in truth. Lewis said it this way: "What are facts without interpretation?" (*Surprised by Joy* 121). All facts must be interpreted, and all interpretations regarding facts are matters of either truth or falsehood. When our interpretations of the facts are accurate, what is inside our heads is *true* knowledge. When our interpretations of the facts are inaccurate, what is inside our heads is false knowledge. And, of course, we can invent facts for our own purposes, which makes our knowledge not only false but manipulatively so.

But none of this is the main point of this book. What I intend to pursue includes epistemological concerns but more as well. It begins, of course, with saying that I intend to explore an aspect of C. S. Lewis's thought. Lewis was perhaps the most important Christian writer of the 1900s, his book *Mere Christianity* perhaps the most influential work of theology in that century. Born in Northern Ireland in 1898, Lewis was raised in the church but lost his faith in his teen years. He was educated primarily in England, studied at Oxford (earning three degrees), fought in World War I, and then became a Fellow of Magdalen College, Oxford, where he taught some philosophy and primarily Medieval and Renaissance literature. Lewis the atheist became Lewis the Idealist, Theist, and then Christian, largely due to the influences of his friends Owen Barfield and J. R. R. Tolkien (author of *The Lord of the Rings*), but also because he *did* pursue truth (and found it in the real). Lewis wrote literary criticism, much of which has stood the test of time, apologetics works in defense of the Christian faith, devotional studies, and science fiction and fantasy for children and adults. His *Chronicles of Narnia* have sold in the millions and been adapted into film. He wrote with style and precision, wrote with a clarity (in both his popular and scholarly work) that was often lacking in his contemporaries. He read widely and remembered everything he read, and he wrote letters in reply to everyone who ever wrote him. He lived within the Modernist world, considered himself something of a "dinosaur" in that world, but wrote in response to that world offering an almost countercultural critique that continues to resonate for twenty-first-century thinkers. And so this is a book about an important idea, but one seen through the lens of Lewis's thought.[3]

The idea, then, is C. S. Lewis's theory of the Real. Lewis was enamored of the Real more than of things *about* the Real. He certainly loved truth and often wrote of it. But for him, truth was about seeing reality. It's not at all an exaggeration to say that Lewis spent a lifetime in pursuit of the Real. He wanted to know it, connect to it, experience it, understand it, live through it.

We can see this point in Lewis's essay, "Meditation in a Toolshed." In the essay, Lewis tells us about a time he was in his toolshed with the door shut. It was dark except for a single beam of light, which dimly lit the space. Lewis noticed that as he looked *at* the beam of light, he saw little of what was around him save the beam itself. But then he stepped into the beam and looked *along* it. And along the beam he saw beyond the dark space into the outside world of grass and trees and sky and the sun illuminating it all. Now Lewis would say both points of view are important. Sometimes we need to step outside the beam and look *at* it as a psychologist might study the way young people act when they fall in love. But sometimes we need to step into the beam and look *along* it. People will learn something *about* love by staring at it but only by stepping

---

3. Over twenty biographies have been written about Lewis (including an autobiography, *Surprised by Joy*). I recommend the following: Sayer, *Jack: A Life of C. S. Lewis*; Duriez, *C. S. Lewis: A Biography of Friendship*; and Brown, *A Life Observed*.

into love and going through it will they move beyond the abstract into the reality of love itself ("Meditation in a Toolshed" 53–57).

A key to Lewis's writing success was his practice of using vivid, concrete illustrations to explain a difficult concept. Following his lead, I'll share how I explain the idea of stepping into the beam of experiential knowledge to my college students. I ask them to think about one of their favorite films: "Pick a movie that has a powerful effect on you—a film that makes you cry or moves you to deep thought. Now imagine that you're taking a film class and your teacher tells you to write a paper on your favorite movie. Finally! For once in your life, you get to write a paper you're really going to enjoy. You go back to the dorm and tell your roommate you're writing your paper on Christopher Nolan's *Interstellar*. Your roommate, who is also taking the class, says, 'That's great, I'll write about that movie too.' Thinking you've found a kindred spirit, you ask, 'You mean you've seen it!' 'No,' he says. 'Okay,' you say, 'We can watch it together.' Then your roommate says something crazy: 'Nah, I don't really have time to watch it, I'll just look at a plot summary of it on *Wikipedia* and read the section on "themes" and write my paper from that.' Your jaw drops. You can't believe this guy is serious. How could anyone really get the profound message to be had from such a powerful film by just looking *at* a summary of it and reading a bunch of *abstract* notes about it? The only way to really learn from that movie, to get anything out of that film, is to experience the full *reality* of the movie itself. You have to watch it." The point again: truth about reality is great. But *Reality itself* is so much better. And that's what C. S. Lewis believed about everything, including God—who, for Lewis, was the most Real thing there is.

This will also be a book, then, about Lewis's Christian vision. There is a theoretical—a theological—element in this study but there are practical elements as well: an interest in knowing reality, an understanding of the importance of discerning what that knowledge means for the actions we take in life, a pursuit of the real on multiple levels—in multiple natures, and a pursuit of God that brings us to what is for Lewis the limits of theory and knowing.

Some things, Lewis would say, can't be known *about* at all—God more than any other. In the biblical text, Job wanted to know why he had suffered. God could have told him that Satan had asked to put Job to the test. But God didn't. We know the events of Job 1, but Job never did. Instead, God appeared to Job and started painting pictures of the creation and God's relationship to it. "Look at what I've done," God says. And looking (four chapters worth) is enough for Job. He says, "My ears had heard of you / but now my eyes I have seen you. / Therefore I despise myself / and repent in dust and ashes" (Job 42:5–6 NIV). God doesn't teach Job abstract truths, God shows him the reality of who God is. In the same way, Jesus could have given the publican a straightforward, abstract truth statement when the man asked him, "Who is my neighbor?" Instead, he told him the story of the Good Samaritan (Luke 10:25–37). He didn't *say*. He *showed*. Can any deep suffering be overcome through theological truth statements? Even Lewis, in trying to do so in his first book of apologetics, *The Problem of Pain*, writes that while truth can help with understanding, talking about pain as an object of speculation has its limitations (see Lewis's preface; *Pain* 9–10). He suggests elsewhere that we can't really know pain except when we're in it ("Myth Became Fact" 66). The problem is more obvious when we compare *The Problem of*

Pain with Lewis's later work, *A Grief Observed*, a book Lewis wrote after his wife's death. To know about pain is a pale shadow in comparison to encountering the thing itself. This, as I said, is also what Lewis believed about God.

God, says Lewis, is not primarily interested in having us know about him. God wants us to know God *himself*. Lewis says that anyone who wants to give thought to understanding him would want the best ideas about God—in terms of accuracy and clarity—on the market (*Mere Christianity* 135). But the reality of God is so much more important than our ideas about God. This is Lewis's point in his Narnia stories when he repeats that Aslan is not a "tame lion" (in *The Lion, the Witch and the Wardrobe* and especially in *The Last Battle*). God can't be pinned down. God can't be studied like a subject in science. Regarding the nature of faith, Lewis says that if faith in Christ doesn't involve listening and acting on the things he said, then it's not faith. It's just "intellectual acceptance of some theory about Him" (*Mere Christianity* 131). And regarding our failure to understand the three-personal nature of God, he says, "You may ask, 'If we cannot imagine a three-personal Being, what is the good of talking about Him?' Well, there isn't any good talking about Him. The thing that matters is being actually drawn into that three-personal life" (143). And again, regarding the nature of a prayer relationship with God, Lewis writes that however much we think we are praying to God—the real God as God really is—we must always remind ourselves that our thoughts and God's reality aren't the same. He says that God is iconoclastic—God constantly breaks our images of who God is. And so, every idea we form in our heads about God is ultimately shattered by God in mercy. The best result people could hope for in prayer in their understanding of God would be to come away from it "thinking, 'But I never knew before. I never dreamed'" (*Letters to Malcolm* 82). But then

Lewis is suggesting here that, in prayer, there is a chance we can encounter at least a part of who and what God really is. To enter into relationship with God as opposed to only thinking about God—that's what leads to more than abstract truths; that's what leads to a knowledge of the Real.

In this book, then, we will overview C. S. Lewis's theory of *Reality*. We will learn that God is the most real thing there is. We will learn that reality is a thing we experience and that much of what we know (correct or false) comes through experience. We will learn that there is a hierarchy to reality and ultimately that reality is sacramental. We will learn that there is a moral reality, that *ought* is as concrete as *is* in Lewis's thinking. And we will see something of what Heavenly Reality might be like. What I won't be doing is claiming that a theory of reality is the key to all of Lewis's thinking. Lewis's mind is too big to be reduced to a single topic. But I do think the Real is one of Lewis's keys, and so I propose a study that might enrich our understanding of C. S. Lewis in the same way that the study of an artist's use of a single pigment might give us new insight into his total body of work.

Acknowledgments

My sincerest thanks goes to Diana Glyer, who not only wrote the foreword to this book but helped make it a better project in the end with her keen reader's eye and expert suggestions for improving both the style and content. I'm grateful to my wife Becky for her support through the process and to my fellow members of the Appalachian Lewis Consortium (Crystal, Devin, William) for always making it so much fun. Finally, I thank Susan Wadsworth-Booth, Mary Young, the adoption committee, and everyone else at Kent State University Press for making this book a reality.

Permissions

The Screwtape Letters by C.S. Lewis © copyright 1942 C.S. Lewis Pte. Ltd.

Miracles by C.S. Lewis © copyright 1947, 1960 C.S. Lewis Pte. Ltd.

Till We Have Faces by C.S. Lewis © copyright 1956 C.S. Lewis Pte. Ltd.

Manuscript on Prayer by C.S. Lewis © copyright C.S. Lewis Pte. Ltd.

Extracts reprinted by permission.

CHAPTER I

The Truest Philosophy

The primary synonym for the word *reality* in Lewis's works is the word *fact,* a word that Lewis uses in a straightforward, consistent manner; however, other synonyms that Lewis uses, including *history, myth,* and *nature,* don't carry quite the comprehensive scope of the words *reality* and *fact* (see the appendix for summary examples, citations, and discussions on these various words and more). In the chapters ahead, we will take up these various words to lesser or greater extents, but here we begin with the almost synonymous connection for Lewis between the words *reality* and *fact.*

In *Miracles,* Lewis writes that "concrete, individual, determinate things do now exist"; these "are not mere principles or generalities or theorems, but things—facts—real, resistant existences" (115). He shortly thereafter refers to the "brute fact of existence, the fact that it is actually there and is itself." Most importantly he refers to God as the "basic, original, self-existent Fact" (43) and as an "uncreated and unconditioned reality" (105). From this and other references it is clear that when Lewis is speaking of fact, he is speaking of reality. But Lewis also writes that a "complete philosophy must get in *all* the facts" (58), later referring to the "rightful demand that all reality should be consistent and systematic" (83).

Lewis's approach to knowledge is as simple (and complicated) as this demand that, whatever system of thought we
develop, it must take all of reality into account. This idea is
central to his argument against pure materialism. In *Miracles*
Lewis says that what the "Naturalist believes is that the ultimate Fact, the thing you can't go behind, is a vast process
in space and time which is *going on of its own accord*" (14).
In other words, the ultimate fact is *Nature*. But Lewis does
not accept this, arguing that "Nature is a *creature*, a created
thing, with its own particular tang or flavour" (87). As such,
it is created fact. He claims that "God is basic Fact" (121), that
the "Supernaturalist agrees with the Naturalist that there
must be something which exists in its own right; some basic Fact" (15). The Supernaturalist, moreover, believes that
facts fall into two categories. In the first category is the "One
Thing which is basic and original, which exists on its own."
In the second category are things that exist because of the
One Thing (God): "The one basic Thing has caused all other
things to be. It exists on its own; they exist because it exists"
(15). Lewis says that the Naturalist thinks nature is "the ultimate and self existent Fact" (87), whereas the Supernaturalist thinks "God is basic Fact or Actuality" and "the source of
all other facthood" (121). Elsewhere in *Miracles* Lewis calls
God the "fountain of facthood" (117). This is a prime example of Lewis's approach to knowing, that is, his epistemology. Begin at the foundations of reality: what is the most real
thing there is? what is the ultimate fact? The direction of
everything else we think begins here.

One of the more famous Lewis quotes is "I believe in
Christianity as I believe that the sun has risen, not only because I see it, but because by it I see everything else" ("Is
Theology Poetry?" 82). In other words, for Lewis, Christianity accounts for all the facts. If any argument can be made

for the greatness of Lewis's thinking, it is this: he pursued the truth with all his heart, mind, and strength. What he came to realize is that every time he was certain he'd found the truth, some experience of reality told him he didn't have all the facts. He discusses his search at length in his autobiography *Surprised by Joy*, and he summarizes the process in his afterword to *The Pilgrim's Regress*. Having tried so many avenues to what he thought was the answer to all his questions, he concluded that every one of them (until he became a Christian) was wrong (203; see chapter 2 on "Desire").

The examples I've created below may help make this point more concrete:

1. Some people feel the stirrings of romantic love and think that finding the perfect mate will make all their dreams come true (and if not the perfect mate, then the perfect night(s) of sex). But the satisfaction, however fulfilling it is, doesn't last. It disappoints, and the result is often separation, divorce, multiple partners, multiple marriages, and disillusionment. These people are missing some of the facts (like the fact that the only true fulfillment of love in reality is to be found in Love himself).

2. Athletes are convinced that victory will satisfy their desires. Eventually their shelves (or more likely some boxes packed into the attic) are filled with dust-gathering trophies they don't even look at anymore, and they think seriously about a career change or how their limbs aren't as capable as they were ten years ago.

3. All any of us need to make the American dream come true is a house with a two-car garage, two bathrooms, three bedrooms, a fenced-in backyard, a dog, 2.3 kids, hardwood floors, furniture updated every five to ten years; cell phones, TVs, computers, gaming consoles and other

technology that aren't more than five years old; a couple of cars; a closet full of clothes (none of which are more than five years old); an open-concept, decked-out kitchen with that latest thing from that strangely European-sounding company; a 401k plus another account for the kids' college education; three to four vacation weeks a year to exotic locales; enough money to eat out three or four times a week; closets and attics full of stuff we absolutely had to have, which we then empty out in garage sales to make room for more stuff we absolutely have to have—you get the point. And when none of that satisfies, we go through a thing called midlife crisis because we thought we'd be happy, but we failed to take into account all the facts (like the fact that nothing in this world can ever satisfy the desires of a supernatural human soul).

4. Some religions teach that the way to get to heaven is by doing good. But the facts of experience teach us that we can never live up to our own expectations let alone those of some divine power. We live in a perpetual state of guilt (or denial). Some religions teach that the world is an illusion to be escaped, while others teach that nature is a divine and beautiful thing; however, in both cases, the experience of suffering and horror remind us that the world is painfully real, and nature is at best indifferent toward human survival.

5. Atheists say there is no God, but they cannot explain (anywhere near as effectively as theists can) the legitimacy of reason, the existence of a sense of goodness and the conscience that convicts us of it, our belief in meaning, the significance of love, and especially the recognition and experience of beauty in the world. Their philosophy doesn't cover all the facts of reality.

In short, then, Lewis believed that if we want to get at the truth and if we want the answers to life, we've got to come to know Reality—all that is real, every aspect, every fact, every experience we can have.[1]

1. Two Lewis scholars who have written on Lewis's emphasis on reality are worth review: Honda, *The Imaginative World of C. S. Lewis*; and Payne, *Real Presence*.

CHAPTER 2

Reality and Desire

Is Reality Really Real?

The ideas that Lewis had about reality as I described them in the last chapter were not always what he thought. Lewis's view of the nature of reality changed—developed—especially in his early years. Students of Lewis often divide this development into periods. Though there may be more such periods in Lewis's thinking (I'm going to pass over his childhood, for example), I'm going to focus on three: Lewis the atheist-materialist, Lewis the antinaturalist or Idealist, and Lewis the Supernaturalist.

Lewis the atheist makes himself visible in his earliest use of the term *fact*. In 1916, the young C. S. Lewis had been an atheist for several years and had become a demythologizer. In a letter to Arthur Greeves, Lewis writes that Jesus was a historical person as were Buddha and King Arthur, but that the miraculous claims about him are mythological. He concludes that "most legends have a kernel of fact in them somewhere" (October 18, 1916, in *They Stand Together* 137). This first significant use of the word *fact* in Lewis's writing is made as a contrast to *legend* or *mythology*.

Early on, however, Lewis began flirting with Idealism. According to Walter Hooper, Lewis became very interested in philosophy in 1917, at which time he began reading the philosophy of Berkeley (Hooper xxix). In July 1917, Lewis writes to Greeves, saying that he'd read three dialogues by Berkeley that prove God's existence "by dis-proving the existence of matter" (July 24, 1917, in *They Stand Together* 196). Thus began a gradual process that led Lewis to the conviction that physical nature was evil (Hooper xxxi). By 1918, while fighting in the trenches in World War I, Lewis could write to Greeves, "out here, where I see spirit continually dodging matter (shells, bullets, animal fears, animal pains) I have formulated my equation Matter=Nature=Satan. And on the other side Beauty, the only spiritual and not-natural thing that I have yet found" (May 23, 1918, in *They Stand Together* 214). This is an easy point to miss. Lewis believed that physical reality was a bad thing. Where we think of atheists as primarily materialists—people who believe that there is nothing except the universe—the C. S. Lewis who was still more than a decade away from believing in God did not hold to any kind of pure materialism for very long. And his experiences of Beauty "on the other side" were significant to his development (as we'll see below).

Clearly, Lewis's view of reality was evolving. It had occurred to him, for example, that there might be something more to a tree than its material substance, "some indwelling spirit behind the matter of the tree" (May 29, 1918, in *They Stand Together* 217), and he wondered if the idea of the Dryad was truer than a purely material approach to nature. To say that Lewis became an Idealist is no small thing. The move from Atheism to Idealism was no less than a recognition of the existence of spiritual reality—something really there that transcended the physical. By 1918 he was becoming convinced of the existence of Spirit just outside of time and space that is not the creator of matter but its "great enemy," and that "Beauty is the call of the spirit" of that unknown transcendent thing "to the spirit in us" (May 29, 1918, in *They Stand Together* 217).

Lewis's eventual journey to believing in God and heaven— the existence of supernatural realities—followed well-thought-out logical steps. He believed in pursuing philosophical truth and in acting on that truth. There was, however, a second road simultaneous to the first that Lewis took on his way to seeing a Christian vision of reality. The first road was philosophical, the second was imaginative. One came through reason, the other came through a certain set of experiences that were invoked most by beauty in nature and art.

Desire

Very early in his life, Lewis experienced something powerful. The imaginative Lewis was drawn into aesthetic experience, an experience he defined as an intense longing for some unnamed thing.[1] He first encountered this experience in the memory of a model of a garden his brother had made when Lewis was a child. For years afterward (and throughout the rest of his life), he was haunted by a desire for some nameless thing, which he thought he would find in one source or

---

1. While Lewis encountered this experience early in life, referring to it in terms of "longing," "Joy," and "Sehnsucht," he also connected it to a concept of the Numinous as identified in Rudolf Otto's *The Idea of the Holy: An Inquiry into the Non-rational Factor in the Idea of the Divine and Its Relation to the Rational*. Lewis recommended the book as one of the top ten most influential books in his life and cited it in *The Problem of Pain*.

another—in nature, in romance, in fantastic literature, especially myth and most especially Norse myth. But all of these turned out to be mere shadows of the Transcendent Other—the God—which he would ultimately recognize as the true source of his longing. Early on, however, when he encountered Transcendent Desire, the longing was accompanied by such intense, sweet pleasure that Lewis gave it a name: *Joy.* And he found that Joy, though it was an unfulfilled desire, was a greater pleasure in the wanting than any fulfilled desires he might experience in any other part of his life.

At first, as noted above, Lewis looked to the variety of his experiences—of beauty in nature or of mythic, wondrous literature—as the objects he was longing for. For a while he even thought the object of his longing might be romantic love and the sexual satisfaction that goes with it. Eventually he came to realize none of these things would fulfill his longing. The inexpressible, unattainable thing he wanted was so utterly Other that he came to realize it must be God. Lewis concluded in *Mere Christianity* that "If I find in myself a desire which no experience in this world can satisfy, the most probable explanation is that I was made for another world" (121). I'll return to this idea, but what is significant here is the idea that our knowledge of the real may have two important qualities:

1. It may come from experiences that at first seem to be very subjective—experiences it may be difficult to prove to others or to trust in ourselves as anything other than our own wishes. In Lewis's thinking, such knowledge is so completely real that it cannot be a matter of mere mental states, brain chemistry, or emotion. We may use the experiences to find the wrong things to worship—nature, art, romance—but if we follow them to their right conclusion, they will lead us to God.

2. To know the real is not only to know facts about the physical universe. Reality is so much more than what can be written down, discovered by careful experimentation, or reasoned to by logic.

Let's now take Joy further to see its implications on that Reality called Heaven and human desire for it. In "The Weight of Glory," Lewis takes his experience of longing and applies it to the biblical concept of glory. He speaks first about the longing people feel: a desire for a "far-off country" that we refuse to admit we long for. A desire so secret that we take revenge on it by passing it off as nostalgia or labeling it *Romanticism* or attributing it to the foolishness of youth. Stranger still is the paradox that the desire is for something we've never experienced, but our experiences constantly suggest it. He then says, "Our commonest expedient is to call it beauty and behave as if that had settled the matter" ("The Weight of Glory" 6–7).

Next Lewis considers the promises of heaven, the chief of which is that we will enter into God's glory. He notes the strangeness of this promise since *Glory* seems to reference fame (a not-so-Christian virtue) and, well, bright light ("The Weight of Glory" 11). He explains the former in terms of God's eternal recognition. Earthly fame is vain because it fades. The glory of heaven is the glory of being acknowledged by the eternal, infinite recognition of God. It is to be told (as in Christ's parable) "well done, good and faithful servant" once and for all unto eternity (11–12). The glory we associate with appearance—especially of light—Lewis connects to beauty, and this takes us back to his concept of *longing* and *desire*, which produces Joy—the Joy we experience when we encounter beauty. This is a thing we long for; this is a thing we desire: to experience beauty in the world that comes from beyond the world.

Ecclesiastes 3:11 tells us that God "has made everything beautiful in its time. He has also set eternity in the human heart." This "setting" and its association with beauty find voice in Lewis's concept of *Longing*. In *Mere Christianity*, Lewis tells us that creatures do not have desires if such desires can't be satisfied. That babies are born hungry means that food exists somewhere in the world. That ducklings are born wanting to swim means water exists as well. So too, then, with sexual desire and various other pleasures. What then if we find a desire in ourselves that nothing in the world can satisfy? As noted above, Lewis says it probably means we were created for "another world" (*Mere Christianity* 121). The desire within can be satisfied by no earthly pleasures, but not because we're being cheated. Instead, it's because those pleasures are meant to wake us up to the thing we really want. It is, as Lewis says, a thing we've never had: everything that has "ever deeply possessed your soul have been but hints of it—tantalising glimpses, promises never quite fulfilled, echoes that died away just as they caught your ear. But if it should really become manifest . . . you would know it. Beyond all possibility of doubt you would say 'Here at last is the thing I was made for'" (*The Problem of Pain* 146).

In "The Weight of Glory," Lewis admits that the idea is rather sentimental. As noted before, he speaks of a "far-off country," but he does so with "shyness," afraid of acting indecently as he works to tear open the deep-seated secret we all share, the one we take revenge on by calling it "Nostalgia" (6). We are, in fact, embarrassed to even speak of the longing because it's a desire for something we haven't actually experienced, but neither can we hide the desire because it is constantly being suggested in our experiences (6–7). And so we call it being romantic or being nostalgic, or we label it as an aesthetic experience—an experience of beauty—and think we've got a grasp on it. But the happy memories of nostalgia, the romantic feelings for a lover, or the experience of beauty are not the thing we really want; "they are only the scent of a flower we have not found, the echo of a tune we have not heard, news from a country we have never visited" (7).

As noted earlier, Lewis experienced this longing for a yet unnamed object throughout his life. He said it was "an unsatisfied desire which is itself more desirable than any other satisfaction. I call it Joy" (*Surprised by Joy* 17–18), and it is something to be distinguished from either "Happiness" or "Pleasure" in that it remains a desire unfulfilled, yet an experience we deeply long to have again (18). Pleasures might be an indicator of it; they might lead to an experience of the longing called Joy, but in the end all such pleasures ever reveal is that they are not the thing truly being desired (169–70). Lewis calls the idea a romantic one "because inanimate nature and marvellous literature were among the things that evoked it" throughout his early life (*Pilgrim's Regress* 202). Lewis came to understand that the same things did not evoke this experience in other people, but he tries to describe it so that anyone can recognize it:

> The experience is one of intense longing. It is distinguished from other longings by two things. In the first place, though the sense of want is acute and even painful, yet the mere wanting is felt to be somehow a delight. Other desires are felt as pleasures only if satisfaction is expected in the near future; hunger is pleasant only while we know (or believe) that we are soon going to eat. But this desire, even when there is no hope of possible satisfaction, continues to be prized, and even to be preferred to anything else in the world, by those who have once felt it. This hunger is better than any other fullness. (*Regress* 202)

Lewis even notes that if the experience of desire disappears for a while, it can in itself become desired. More peculiar than this experience of desire itself, however, is the mystery of its object. Few people ever understand what the object is. If a child has the experience while he is looking at hills in the distance, he thinks that what he wants is to be there. If it happens in a wonderful memory, he will desire to be back in those better times. Some years later, it may come when he's reading a great adventure story or when he sees a beautiful woman and longs for her, but none of these objects is the thing he truly desires (*Regress* 203). What is it that he, that we, are all longing for?

Lewis's answer in the sermon, "The Weight of Glory," exists within his definition of glory. For Lewis, glory means entering into God's beauty (16). In *Miracles*, Lewis recalls from his reading of classical poetry that "brightness" had more of an appeal to ancient peoples than it does for modern humans (*Miracles* 73). He associates light with beauty in his own letters: writing to his friend Mary about a long spell of fog, he notes that he misses the "lights" and even their accompanying "shadows . . . which make up so much of the beauty of the world" (December 25, 1958, in *Letters to an American Lady* 80). And a month later he describes a winter beauty: "bright, pale sunshine," which his wife calls "'arctic light' . . . still air, and just that sprinkling of hoar-frost which makes everything sparkle like sugar" (January 26, 1959, in *Letters to an American Lady* 81). Lewis describes the pleasures of beauty in *Letters to Malcolm* as "shafts of the glory as it strikes our sensibility" (89), or "'patches of Godlight' in the woods of our experience" (91). In "Dungeon Grates" beauty has a power that can "build a bridge of light" (*Collected Poems* 184; line 19) to bring the human soul safely out of the pains of earthly life to encounter a greater light. Then, when this miraculous moment fades, we hold onto our vision of it, and remember that we are not merely mortal and so can bear every trial that life hereafter brings (184; lines 27–37). We can do this because "we have seen the Glory" (185; line 40). An artist in *The Great Divorce* wants very much to capture the beauty of the heavenly landscape, a beauty that he first recognized existed in his love for light (see *Divorce* 83–87). On earth he was a successful painter because he had been able to catch "glimpses of Heaven in the earthly landscape" and show it to others in his art (83). But what started him on his aesthetic endeavors was a love for light: "Light itself was your first love" a heavenly friend reminds him (84).[2] For Lewis, light is a symbol of beauty, beauty is a revelation of glory, and glory is made, in part, of light.

But Lewis goes even further in "The Weight of Glory." We want so much more than just to "see beauty" as wonderful as that is. "We want . . . to be united with the beauty we see, to pass into it, to receive it into ourselves, to bathe in it to become part of it." Lovers of nature understand this desire. They don't want to just look at nature (16), they "want to absorb it into themselves, to be coloured through and through by it." We will bathe in glory just as Robin wants to bathe in light in Lewis's "Light" short story,[3] just as the angels do in *Out of the Silent Planet*. God will one day "give us the Morning Star and cause us to put on the splendour of the sun" ("The Weight of Glory" 16–17). To put on God's Glory is to put on God's Light. Heaven is a place where the "Glory flows into everyone, and back from everyone: like light and

2. The inspiration for the artist character in *Divorce* is probably nineteenth-century artist, philosopher, and critic John Ruskin, whose works Lewis read and admired.

3. Originally published as "The Man Born Blind," I published and discussed the story in my first book on Lewis, *Light: C. S. Lewis's First and Final Short Story*.

mirrors" (*Divorce* 86). In *The Great Divorce*, when the only ghost in heaven who chooses to receive the fullness of Being begins his transformation into a wholly *real* soul—a person filled with the weight of God's Glory—that transformation is described in terms of light. He grows "brighter" (111). His face shines with what might be tears or what might only be the "liquid love and brightness . . . which flowed from him" (112). He leaps onto a horse and rides away "like a shooting star," himself "bright," on "into the rose-brightness of that everlasting morning." To be filled with God's Glory is to be filled with light. And it is to have our longings fulfilled.

A balloon isn't much of anything, metaphorically speaking. There's not a lot of reality to it. In fact, it's mostly just air. Take the air out of the balloon and fill it up with water instead. Now there's some substance to it! Now it's a refreshing weapon of attack on a hot summer day when playing with the kids out in the yard. But imagine that balloon is now filled with something more than normal water. There are two scenes in Lewis's fiction in which something like this occurs. The first, in *Perelandra*, is when Ransom touches a bulbous piece of fruit hanging from a tree. To his surprise, the fruit bursts and washes over him, not with a sticky mess but with a greater refreshment than any of us can possibly imagine (*Perelandra* 42). In *The Voyage of the Dawn Treader*, the travelers to the Utter East are refreshed by sweet seawater, which they say feels like drinking liquid light. They don't need to eat food anymore for the water sustains them (*Treader* 248). They've drunk living water as Christ promised the woman at the well (John 4:14). And the joy they're experiencing becomes so intense that it's more than they can stand (*Treader* 258).

Now take the balloon and reshape it. Make it into a balloon animal. Make it into a human shape. Make a single balloon in your imagination that looks like you and fill that balloon with nothing but air. Imagine stepping out into heaven as that thin, empty membrane, like the ghostly people in *The Great Divorce*. There's almost nothing of you there. You're hardly real at all. In fact, there's so little Reality to you that you can't even flatten the grass under your feet as you step on it. In the book, only one ghost moves beyond this stage. When the lizard of lust on the man's shoulder is killed, he changes. He becomes filled with light—not the airy stuff we think of but the dense, solid liquidity of the Glory of God. Full Reality enters into him, and he transforms into a real person for the first time in his life. He is filled with the water, the light, the glory, the beauty of God. He has become Real. That, Lewis would say, is humanity's deepest desire, our deepest longing. That's what we want more than anything this pale world has to offer. In short, central to C. S. Lewis's theory of reality is that you and I aren't yet real enough. And our whole life's pursuit is a pursuit of the greatest Reality of all, not just so that we can find it (him), not just so that we can know it, but so that it can enter into us and we can become, finally, utterly and completely real ourselves.

CHAPTER 3

Encountering the Real through Experience and Imagination

At the time of his conversion, Lewis wrote that "the story of Christ is simply a true myth," one that works on us the way other myths do but with this big difference: "it really happened." To the pagans, God expressed himself through their poets using the images he found there; in Christianity he expresses himself through "'real things'" (October 18, 1931, in *Collected Letters* I: 977). Lewis goes on in the same letter to note a correspondence between this reality and *sensory perception:* "it is *true,* not in the sense of being a 'description' of God (that no finite mind could take in) but in the sense of being the way in which God chooses to (or can) appear to our faculties." So that people may have some limited understanding of God, he chooses to appear to us in the world of "real things" where our senses can perceive his appearance.

In a later chapter, I will identify the view of reality that the Christian Lewis held as *sacramental.* But for now, consider this idea of the "real, resistant existence" of reality and the significance Lewis saw in it regarding our ability to know truth. The atheist Lewis didn't have all the information he needed to explain all of his experiences of reality. Materialism could not explain the existence of beauty nor his pangs of longing. Idealism made the world of his senses less real. As soon as he could believe in God as the ultimate fact, though, he could believe in a creator God who makes a *Nature* apart from himself—a nature with which he is pleased. Real things exist. That is to say, real things are real. And knowing reality for what it is becomes important in Lewis's thinking.

Learning from the (Fictional) Real

The significance of a focus on reality for coming to true knowledge is clear in *Out of the Silent Planet*, which was published in 1938. For Lewis, a good dose of reality corrects false belief. But when I say this in the context of discussing Lewis's first science fiction novel, it raises the question of the relationship between imaginative fiction and reality.

First of all, it's fictional. It's a story that hasn't happened in the real world. Secondly, it's imaginative, and we tend to think that anything having to do with the imagination is unreal. If it comes from the imagination, it is imaginary. If it is imaginary, it is not real. A short response to this from Lewis would be something like this: reality is something we experience (this is the idea of looking "along the beam"). Stories (fictional or historical) are also something we experience—we just do it in our imaginations. A fictional story can put people through honest experiences that take hold of reality, which present qualities of the real. Lewis suggests this idea in the last chapter of *Out of the Silent Planet* in which he says that the story of Ransom's journey, even perceived as fiction, might yet alter the readers' "conception" of reality beyond the Earth from that of "Space" to that of "Heaven" (152). He suggests that fairy stories could correct our emotional responses to religious ritual and imagery by "stripping them of their stained-glass and Sunday school associations" and making them appear in their "real potency," thus stealing "past those watchful dragons" of familiarity and a sense of moral obligation to feel a certain way about church and God ("Sometimes Fairy Stories May Say Best" 37). And in *An Experiment in Criticism*, Lewis suggests that the primary good that literature serves is to "admit us to experiences other than our own" (139), so that we can see reality (and more than reality) "through the eyes of many" (140; see also the discussion of Lewis's essay, "Myth Became Fact" in chapter 4 of this book where Lewis connects mythic storytelling to higher reality as well as the argument from sacrament in chapter 9). Lewis's friend and fellow literary critic and writer J. R. R. Tolkien argued that stories are inventions about reality and therefore true (in his poem "Mythopoeia"). Lewis used the word *truth* in a more technical way than Tolkien did, but he would essentially agree with his friend's statement. For Lewis, his three science fiction books and his fantasy tales made it possible for us to encounter and learn from the real.[1]

In *Out of the Silent Planet*, then, Dr. Elwin Ransom, a philologist, is on vacation when he is kidnapped by Devine and Weston and taken to Malacandra (Mars). Ransom overhears that they have kidnapped him because they believe the sorns (a Malacandrian intelligent species) want a human sacrifice for their god. Upon arrival, Ransom manages to escape from his captors, running away in a panic across the strange Malacandrian landscape.

In his wanderings, Ransom stumbles across another intelligent species, the hrossa (which look like giant seals). From

---

1. Several Lewis studies have explored or synthesized Lewis's literary theory, including Schakel and Huttar's *Word and Story in C. S. Lewis;* Edwards's *A Rhetoric of Reading;* and Schakel's *Imagination and the Arts in C. S. Lewis.*

them he learns the Malacandrian language and something of its history. He learns that the great canals of Malacandra are the only habitable part of the planet. He learns that there is a third intelligent species, the pfifltriggi (they are makers, the sorns thinkers, and the hrossa poets), and that there is a fourth kind of creature, the eldila, not animal at all. One of these incorporeal beings, an eldil, comes to the hrossa and tells them that Ransom must go to the Oyarsa. Ransom hears the eldil speak but, unlike the natives, cannot see it.

After a brief encounter with Weston and Devine, which leaves a hross friend dead, Ransom is sent to Meldilorn, where members of all three species of the planet and many eldila have gathered at the seat of Oyarsa, who Ransom learns is also an eldil, but a ruling one. Ransom learns that every planet in the solar system is ruled by such a spiritual creature, including Earth, called Thulcandra in Malacandrian, which translates as the "Silent Planet." Oyarsa tells Ransom that the Oyarsa of Thulcandra/Earth, the "Bent One" who disobeyed Maleldil the Young (the ruler of the eldila), has been bound within the sphere of his moon's orbit and cannot roam freely about the heavens. The Earth, therefore, is cut off from the other planets and silent because many years ago the Bent One struck out at Malacandra and almost destroyed it.

Oyarsa asks Ransom why he did not come to him before, and Ransom explains Devine's and Weston's designs on him. These two are soon brought before Oyarsa by a hross hunting party and made to explain themselves. They do not see Oyarsa, however, and believe that an old hross is a medicine man for these primitive peoples, throwing his voice like a ventriloquist. Weston tries to explain his ideal of the survival of the human species through conquest of the galaxy. He loves human life and wishes to see it continue forever, even if that means destroying other sentient creatures so that humanity can survive. Weston, however, proves to be ridiculous because of his poor grasp of the Malacandrian language and his insistence that the old hross is actually speaking to him. Oyarsa realizes that each of these men, Ransom included, is bent in his own way and demands that they leave at once. He gives them the exact amount of time they need to return home and warns that their ship will then be destroyed. The trio returns safely to Earth, and the ship disintegrates as promised.

Out of the Silent Planet is largely the story of Ransom learning to overcome fear through the revitalization of his imagination. This can only occur, however, by his exposure to the facts of Martian reality. The first evidence of his misinformed view occurs in chapter 5 when he learns that he is to be given to the Sorns. His reaction is one of terror as he imagines the impossible juxtaposition of monstrous body parts; his fear of insects and snakes, of things that squash and squelch, fill him with fear. But then he thinks the actuality will be worse than what he imagines. It would be an unearthly "Otherness" beyond anything he could conjure in his mind (Out of the Silent Planet 35).

Just why Ransom is so terrified, and where the images he has conjured up come from, is explained a few lines above this text: "He had read his H. G. Wells and others. His universe was peopled with horrors such as ancient and mediaeval mythology could hardly rival." Ransom's view of reality is false, based on fictional ideas and images—suppositions of what life on other worlds must be like based on a naturalistic world view of the universe.

Ransom's first moment of rehabilitation occurs when he sees the Malacandrian landscape and realizes unexpectedly that it is beautiful. It strikes him as unusual that the thought had never occurred to him that he might encounter beauty here: "The same peculiar *twist of imagination* which led him to people the universe with monsters had somehow taught him to expect nothing on a strange planet except rocky desolation or else a network of nightmare machines" (42; emphasis added). At first it doesn't help much, for Ransom next sees sorns for the first time and, though he finds them "quite unlike the horrors his imagination had conjured up," they nevertheless appeal to "an earlier, almost infantile, complex of fears. Giants–ogres–ghosts–skeletons: those were its key words" (47).

Ransom's fleeing the sorns and meeting his first hross begins his imaginative transformation. It happens because he realizes that the creature is speaking. As a philologist (one who studies words and languages), he is swept away and his imagination leaps beyond whatever circumstances or wild emotions he is feeling. The chance to make a "grammar" of Martian language is overwhelming to a professor of linguistics like himself. From a nonterrestrial language, he might even discover the essence of language, the organizing archetypes behind all languages (55). The image of heroic discovery, coupled with his experience of reality as it is, allows Ransom to correctly envision the world around him. Ransom learns to love the hrossa as a noble species. He is more reluctant with the sorns, but even his vision of them is restored by his exposure to fact: "The grace of their movement, their lofty stature, and the softened glancing of the sunlight on their feathery sides, effected a final transformation in Ransom's feelings towards their race" (101). Where before he had envisioned them with words like "Ogre," he now imagined them more like "Titans" or "Angels."[2]

2. An imaginative vision of the real was significant to Lewis, and though he admired the classical vision ("Titans") of Greek and Roman mythology, his favorite comprehensive vision of the cosmos was the medieval vision (Angels), which he taught and then collected into his pub-

By the time Ransom comes to confront Oyarsa, he is no longer afraid of meeting a monster (118). There he admits that his problem on that world has been one of fear, and this fear had been evoked by imaginings that did not correspond to the real: Ransom explains that he was afraid: "The tellers of tales in our world make us think that if there is any life beyond our own air it is evil" (121). The Oyarsa agrees with Ransom's self-analysis, telling him that he will be ready to go to God when he becomes more courageous (123). This is the essence of his journey, as Oyarsa explains: "You are guilty of no evil, Ransom of Thulcandra, except a little fearfulness. For that, the journey you go on is your pain, and perhaps your cure: for you must be either mad or brave before it is ended" (142).

Ransom returns home to discover that he has overcome much of his fear through an experiential (i.e., exposure to reality) rehabilitation of his imagination. The emphasis on fact in the novel shows that Lewis's approach to knowledge and spiritual growth is grounded in reality; if we would know truly, we must know the Real.

---

lished study, *The Discarded Image*, and which he smuggles into his science fiction trilogy. Among the most comprehensive medieval thinkers who influenced Lewis (and worth the contemporary reader's attention), then, are Aquinas and Dante. Lewis's two-volume copy of Aquinas's *Summa Theologica* has underlining in it from beginning to end, suggesting that Lewis read the *Summa* from cover to cover. He was an avid reader of Dante's *Divine Comedy* as well (taught and wrote on it and critiqued Dorothy Sayers's translation of Dante, offering high praise).

CHAPTER 4

The Apologetical Decade

In the late 1930s and throughout the 1940s, Lewis the Christian strove to systematize his views of Fact/Reality. He hints at doing so in *Silent Planet*. He does so more directly in *The Problem of Pain* (1940), *The Screwtape Letters* (1942), *The Abolition of Man* (1943), "Myth Became Fact" (1944), *The Great Divorce* (1945), most thoroughly in the books that make up *Mere Christianity* (originally 1941–44), and in *Miracles* (1947).

The Problem of Pain

The Problem of Pain begins with the atheist's view of the universe as a place of horror and pain, barely capable of supporting life (13–14). The Christian response to this view as a reason for doubting the existence of God is, first of all, to agree. The universe seems a terrible place. But if so, Lewis asks, then how did human beings come to attribute to the universe any actions of a wise and loving God in the first place (15)? The universe as humanity experiences it can never have been the cause for religious belief. Such belief must have arisen from another source. Lewis considers the problem of pain by first embracing its reality. What follows is an argument based on the facts of physical existence. Rather than glossing over the difficulties that the universe presents, Lewis argues that the Christian system is the only one that embraces all the facts.

Lewis makes his methodology clear. If one looks at the "facts of experience" from the atheist's point of view (21), there is no explanation for the rise of a moral impulse, nor especially for the human reaction of awe toward the universe, what Lewis calls the "Numinous" (20)—this idea takes us back to Lewis's experience of Joy. There is no logical connection between those experiences that cause physical fear and those that produce dread and awe. The experience of the numinous is a "sheer jump" that could never be produced by the "physical facts and logical deductions from them" (20). Here is a clear example of Lewis's fact-based approach to argument. One looks at the facts and then makes logical deductions from them. What he concludes is that, since there are no facts in nature that explain human beings' experience of awe, there must be "a direct experience of the really supernatural, to which the name Revelation might properly be given" (20–21). The general principle being applied here is, as noted above, argument by deduction, which considers all the facts. Lewis's subsequent explanation of the problem of pain, then, proceeds from the facts of reality.[1]

The Screwtape Letters

The Screwtape Letters was first published serially in 1941 and then as a book in 1942. It consists of a series of letters written

---

1. A variety of epigraphs at the beginning of the various chapters in *Pain* indicate the variety of Lewis's reading. Among the classical works quoted that Lewis references as most influential or that he cites regularly in his works and letters are MacDonald's *Unspoken Sermons*, Pascal's *Pensees*, and the *Theologia Germanica*.

by a fictional demon, Uncle Screwtape, to his nephew and novice tempter Wormwood. In the letters, the elder demon tries to instruct the younger on how best to tempt his "patient" or human to sin. Screwtape's opening salvo (in letter 1) includes an attack on the human's sense of reality, arguing that Wormwood should try to get the human to avoid thinking and instead to focus on the "stream of his immediate sense experiences" (think of the constant bombardment of mass media, especially smartphone media, on people today). "Your business," says Screwtape, "is to fix his attention on the stream. Teach him to call it 'real life' and don't let him ask what he means by 'real'" (*Screwtape* 2).

In letter 3, Screwtape teaches Wormwood how best to make his "patient's" prayers powerless. In praying for family members, for example, it's important to have the human pray for his imaginary conception of the people he knows, not the actual people. Wormwood should try to "make the imaginary person daily less and less like the real" one (12). Eventually, this could then lead to the human treating his family members horribly while yet praying dutifully for them, "from impassioned prayer for a wife's or son's 'soul' to beating or insulting the real wife or son without a qualm" (13).

At the end of letter 6, Screwtape provides a theoretical model for the practice of separating real action from imagined love. He describes humans as a series of concentric circles at the center of which is the will (where actual action takes place). In the next circle is the intellect, followed by the outer circle, which Lewis here calls the "fantasy" but by which he means something like a thoughtless imagination. I exemplify Screwtape's point in this way: if you've ever watched a powerful movie in which you experienced some act of human nobility, where characters acted with sacrificial love toward others, you may have experienced a strong sense of satisfaction from the film. But did it make you act differently toward others? I've often said that one of the big dangers of film is "vicarious compassion." Movies give us the ability to feel good, compassionate feelings toward people (who are really just actors in a movie), after which, having these feelings satisfied, we don't actually do anything nice (let alone sacrificial) for any real people. Screwtape urges Wormwood to push his human's "virtues" (like "benevolence") out into his imagination, as far away from his "will" as possible. Then the patient will think he's a compassionate person when in reality he is not (28).

Screwtape's most profound statement about reality, however, is to be found in letter 30. The book is set during World War II, when London was being bombed. The elder demon tells his novice that wartime is probably not the best circumstance for an intellectual attack on the man's faith. Instead, there is a good emotional attack worth trying:

"It turns on making him *feel*, when first he sees human remains plastered on a wall, that this is 'what the world is *really* like' and that all his religion has been a fantasy. You will notice that we have got them completely fogged about the meaning of the word 'real.' They tell each other, of some great spiritual experience, 'All that really happened was that you heard some music in a lighted building'; here 'Real' means the bare physical facts, separated from the other elements in the experience they actually had. On the other hand, they will also say 'It's all very well discussing that high dive as you sit here in an armchair, but wait till you get up there and see what it's really like': here 'real' is being used in the opposite sense to mean, not the physical facts (which they know already while discussing the matter in armchairs) but the emotional effect those facts will have on a human consciousness. Either application of the word could be defended; but our business is to keep the two going at once so that the emotional value of the word 'real' can be placed now on one side of the account, now on the other, as it happens to suit us ... Thus in birth the blood and pain are 'real', the rejoicing a mere subjective point of view; in death, the terror and ugliness reveal what death 'really means'. The hatefulness of a hated person is 'real' ... but the loveliness of a loved person is merely a subjective haze concealing a 'real' core of sexual appetite or economic association. Wars and poverty are 'really' horrible; peace and plenty are mere physical facts about which men happen to have certain sentiments ... Your patient, properly handled, will have no difficulty in regarding his emotion at the sight of human entrails as a revelation of Reality and his emotion at the sight of happy children or fair weather as mere sentiment." (167–69)

It's important to remember here that Screwtape is describing how demons *want* people to use the words *real* and *reality*, not how we *ought* to use those words. The bottom line, though, is that people, including those of deepest Christian faith, are often caught up in this false thinking. Here are some examples I use when trying to explain this to my students:

1. When you told your dad that you wanted to study art or photography, literature or music, he replied, "Well, that's fine, Johnny (or Annie), but that's not gonna help you get ready for the *real world*." What did he mean by the "real world"? He meant the world in which dreams don't come true, you have to pay your own bills, and the job you work must be one you hate. Is that reality?
2. When you or a family member saw something terrible on the news, usually involving a death, one of you said, "Now that's real" or "That's reality." Is reality only the bad things

that happen? When good things happen, aren't they just as real—in fact more so since God is their author?

3. When you go on vacation, inevitably the day comes when you have to head home from Florida, or the Sunday comes when you'll be back at work tomorrow. And you say, "Well, time to go back to the real world." We've come to believe that the restful world, the vacation world, is a lie, and the real world is one of work and drudgery. What's shocking here is the idea that we can even be fooled into lying in our speech, and this false idea—that reality is nothing but the bad in life—can be planted in our heads without our even knowing it.

The Abolition of Man

Lewis's interest in fact/reality is prevalent in *The Abolition of Man* (1943), which begins with his argument against two textbook authors who deny that evaluative statements ("this is bad," "that is beautiful") are about anything other than the speaker's state of mind. What Lewis takes up is a description of nature as qualitative, not merely quantitative. He argues that for most of human history, people believed that the physical universe—and the objects it contained—didn't just receive our intellectual and emotional approval or disapproval, but that it actually merited such responses. The illustration he uses is a famous story from the poet Samuel Taylor Coleridge,[2]

2. Lewis was familiar with Coleridge's *Biographia Literaria*, among other works. In Michael Ward's excellent study, *After Humanity: A Guide to C. S. Lewis's* The Abolition of Man, he sources the waterfall story and discusses Coleridge's thought in lieu of Lewis's argument in *Abolition* (50–52). Lewis's friend Owen Barfield (whom Lewis called the

who was visiting a waterfall one day when one fellow tourist called it "pretty" and another called it "sublime." Coleridge disagreed with the first tourist and agreed with the second one. He agreed with the second one because "he believed inanimate nature to be such that certain responses could be more 'just' or 'ordinate' or 'appropriate' to it than others" (25). In Coleridge's thought, as in Lewis's, the fellow traveler who called the waterfall "sublime" wasn't just describing his own subjective reaction to it, but he was also saying that the waterfall *deserved* his reaction to it—a reaction best labeled by calling it "sublime." So, in *Abolition*, Lewis carefully builds an argument about the nature of Nature, not just human reaction to it. By the book's end, he shows that Nature itself is a vast tapestry of meanings that are real: they exist outside of our subjective perceptions of them, and we need to learn to perceive reality in such a way as to see those self-existent meanings for what they are.

The Chinese, says Lewis, "speak of a great thing (the greatest thing) called the *Tao*. It is the reality beyond all predicates" (28). Synonyms from sources throughout the ages (Platonic, Aristotelian, Stoic, Christian, Oriental) include Nature, the Way, the Road, and the Law (28), as well as Natural Law, Traditional Morality, First Principles of Practical Reason, and first Platitudes (56). Lewis chooses the word *Tao* for simplicity, and to divorce the concept from any accusation of a Western or specifically Christian bias. Lewis is not arguing a mere universal system of rules for moral behavior. The *Tao* is "the doctrine of objective value (29), which is the position that not only are facts/objects/quantities—physical things—true, but that there are attitudes that are

---

best of his unofficial teachers) wrote extensively on Coleridge (much of his work published after Lewis's death)—see especially Barfield's *What Coleridge Thought*.

true (and false) as well in terms of our responses to what we experience in the universe. There are particular attitudes we were designed to have and particular attitudes that objects in reality (like a sublime waterfall) call for.

Lewis rejects the textbook authors' idea that "the world of facts" should be without "one trace of value, and the world of feelings without one trace of truth or falsehood" (30). At the same time, he seems to contradict himself when he rejects any attempt to "base value on fact" (49n). What he actually rejects is the idea that *quantitative facts* about human instinct can yield *qualitative values* (49). But if the facts of reality demand certain emotional responses, how do they do so? Specifically, how does one know what the emotional responses are supposed to be? Lewis's answer involves the concept of *self-evident truth*.

But before looking at Lewis's argument, I want to clarify the problem. It is easy to see the connection between the idea of reality and what *is*. If I say the world is round, that's the reality of the thing. It's a fact. If I say people kill other people, that's an *is* statement. It speaks truthfully to the condition of the world. But if I say people *should not* kill people, I'm no longer talking about what *is*. I'm talking about what *ought to be*. There *is* pain in the world. There *should not be*. An *ought* statement is not the same as an *is* statement. One seems to agree with reality; the other doesn't. But if we claim that ought statements don't seem to be connected to reality as it is, Lewis will answer that we are wrong. He would say that there is an absolute relationship between reality and morality.

In *Abolition*, Lewis argues that values cannot be determined from fact or instinct (52). Where can they be found? Only in the *Tao*, which must be accepted "without question as being to the world of action what axioms are to the world of theory" (53). The values that make up the *Tao* are not conclusions but premises. They cannot be proven by reason; they are "rationality itself"—things so obvious that they neither demand nor admit proof. After all, "If nothing is self-evident, nothing can be proved" (53).

Toward the end of *Abolition*, Lewis turns specifically to attacking the kind of scientism that strips nature of quality, reducing it to quantity. He begins by defining the natural as the "opposite of the Artificial, the Civil, the Human, the Spiritual and the Supernatural" (81). Then, following a modern model, he says nature is space and time the purview of quantity, not quality; that Things are part of nature but consciousness is not; whatever is lacks value and whatever thinks or experiences value is not of nature. And nature can only be explained in terms of "efficient causes," not final ones (81). Lewis then immediately begins poking holes in the absoluteness of this view, looking in several places to join the pairs of opposites.

In the model of modern scientism, which seeks to analyze not for the sake of knowing but for the sake of gaining control, a thing is reduced "to the level of 'Nature' in the sense that we suspend our judgments about it, ignore its final cause (if any), and treat it in terms of quantity" (81). In so doing, we reduce the things of nature to objects without meaning. Trees are neither Dryads nor beautiful objects in themselves; they are merely beams for a house. The stars lose their divinity with astronomy and "the Dying God has no place in chemical agriculture" (82). Some would argue that all that has happened is that we have begun to see the world as it really is. Lewis says that only "small" scientists and unscientific followers of science think so. But the "great minds know very well that the object, so treated, is an artificial abstraction, that something of its reality has been lost" (82). So, Lewis argues that quality, that meaning, is part of true Nature, and if quality, then consciousness, autonomy, value, and final cause are also to be viewed as in some way aspects of Nature. He concludes that the only true understanding of Nature and of humans is within the *Tao*. Only there do "we find the concrete reality in which to participate is to be truly human" (86). For Lewis, concrete reality is reality alive with meaning, responsive to mind, and full of objective moral and aesthetic value.

Mere Christianity

From 1941 to 1944, Lewis delivered a series of talks over the BBC in which he defended and promoted classical Christianity. These series of talks (after subsequent publication) were later revised, combined, and republished as *Mere Christianity*. In these four "books" Lewis's system of fact and reality is more fully delineated.

The first part of *Mere Christianity* takes us to the *Tao* of *Abolition* and the issue of *ought* versus *is*. The inborn law of right and wrong in each person was once "called the Law of Nature" (18), so called because in the past people thought everyone knew it by nature and didn't have to be taught what it was. It is a given, based not on individual or cultural opinion; it is a "real Right and Wrong" (19). And well known about the Law of Nature are "two facts": that people know the Law of Right and Wrong and they cannot obey it (20–21). From these facts, Lewis argues toward the existence of a Law Giver and humanity's guilt before him.

So that his audience is not confused by the term *Law of Nature*, Lewis distinguishes between the modern use of the phrase and his own. Today the laws of nature are descriptions of the way things act in Nature. To say that a falling rock is obeying the law of gravity is just saying that a falling rock is doing what falling rocks always do (28). The rock isn't thinking, "Oh, I've just been dropped from a cliff and now am required by law to fall to the ground." But the "Law of Human Nature" or the "Law of Decent Behaviour" is different. The moral law does not describe what human beings do; rather it describes what we *ought* to do and never completely succeed at doing. In other words, when dealing with people, there's something else playing a part "above and beyond the actual facts" (28). There are facts regarding how people actually act, but there is this other thing telling them how they ought to act.

By introducing the word *ought* into the discussion, Lewis calls up the distinction between prescription and description. The Law of Nature describes how things are; the Law of Human Nature prescribes how things ought to be. And the facts of human behavior (the descriptions) frequently oppose the fact of how people ought to behave. Nevertheless, for Lewis, Natural Law in prescribing *Ought* is as real as any descriptive *Is*. The *Tao* (as Lewis calls it in *The Abolition of Man*) or *Way* is a reality. Is there a way to prove that Lewis is right? The argument that comes to me is one of existential experience: when any of us faces the pain of some terrible evil, our response always includes an element of shock. For parents to learn, for example, that their child is dead will almost certainly make them think such a reality can't be real. Where does that sense of unreality come from if not from the instinctive understanding that real oughtness exists as much as do the hard facts of real events? Our child has died. It never should have happened. It is a fact, but it is not the Way.

Lewis's discussion of reality in *Mere Christianity* next shifts to an emphasis on its hierarchical complexity. That there might be multiple *levels* of reality is first suggested by the idea of descriptive versus prescriptive fact. Lewis moves from mere suggestion to carefully reasoned statement when he contrasts the materialist and religious views of nature (31–32). According to the latter, there is "Something Behind" nature, a reality that cannot be observed in the facts of physical nature and about which one can learn something only by observing human nature (33): Or think of it this way: if a power outside our universe exists, it couldn't reveal itself as just another fact within the universe any more than an architect could be a piece of the house he or she designed. The controlling power could only show itself inside people, influencing them to behave a certain way, and this is exactly what is happening in the Moral Law.

Next then, Lewis wants us to consider what the thing behind the universe might be. He concludes that, of the two things we know, mind and matter, the reality behind must be more like mind than matter since we "can hardly imagine a bit of matter giving instructions" (34), and, as he has already pointed out, "Being behind the universe is intensely interested in right conduct" (37). Lewis rejects those views midway between materialism and religion that attempt to call the "thing behind" names like "Life-Force," or "Emergent Evolution." These attempt to argue in favor of a materialist view while using the language of mind and are simply self-contradictory (34–35).

As the discussion continues, Lewis refuses Pantheism, the view "that the universe almost *is* God" (44). He specifically argues two realities: "God is separate from the world" (45); he is the "Being outside the world" who made it and is "infinitely different from anything else" (55). Natural life (*bios*) mirrors God, is a "kind of symbol or shadow of" him, but lacks "Spiritual life (*zoe*)—the higher and different sort of life that exists in God" (139). Finally, Lewis's great conclusion in *Mere Christianity* about the nature of reality—of fact—is that God is the "rock bottom, irreducible Fact on which all other facts depend" (160). The duality is plain: there is the one Fact of Being, and then there are those facts created by him, utterly dependent upon him for their own being.

Myth Became Fact

The essay "Myth Became Fact" was published in the fall of 1944. Here Lewis focuses on a set of relationships between fact and other concepts, especially the relationship between fact and truth and that between fact and myth. It isn't the first time Lewis has done this. He connected reality to myth in the first two books of his science fiction trilogy. In *Out of the Silent Planet*, the main character, Elwin Ransom, wonders if the distinction humans make between history and mythology might be meaningless beyond Earth (144). And in *Perelandra*, Ransom frequently feels as if he's acting out a myth (42).

Lewis makes several enigmatic statements about fact in the essay, which I want to list first and then try to make sense of. To begin with, he makes a connection between myth and reality and a separation of reality from truth: "What flows into you from the myth is not truth but reality (truth is always *about* something, but reality is that *about which* truth is)." Reality (or fact) is what is; truth is a proposition about fact. We can see from this passage that myth is a vehicle for reality. A little later in the paragraph Lewis notes that myth is not "like direct experience," and in the following paragraph he asserts that myth "comes down from the heaven of legend and imagination to the earth of history" (66).

Next, Lewis describes reality as a "valley of separation" (66n). He suggests, "Myth is the mountain whence all the different streams arise which become truths down here in the valley; *in hac valle abstractionis*" (66). In his next metaphor he says, "if you prefer, myth is the isthmus which connects the peninsular world of thought with that vast continent we really belong to." Then Lewis makes this complicated statement: "Now as myth transcends thought, Incarnation transcends myth." At the center of Christianity is a myth that also happened in history. The universal myth of a god who dies and rises (Balder, Osiris, Adonis) remains a myth but actually happens. It descends from heaven to Earth, from imagination to history. Rather than being located in a nebulous past, it occurs at a specific time and place in human history and produces consequences in the history that follows. And on the next page Lewis adds, "For this is the marriage of heaven and earth: Perfect Myth and Perfect Fact" (67).

These are the six key passages in the essay that touch on the subject of reality. To understand them, we backtrack to the beginning of the essay where Lewis repeats a charge by his friend "Corineus" that modern Christianity is nothing like ancient Christianity, and all that remains of that primitive religion are the trappings of mythology. Lewis thinks this assertion false, but, if it were true, he wonders why Christians continue to hold onto the mythology. It would be much easier for them if they let it go. The answer is that, even if classical Christianity were purely mythical (that is, ahistorical, which Lewis denies), it is that myth that vitalizes and nourishes the religion most of all and endures when philosophical heresies rise and fall. To explain how this is possible, Lewis determines to look more closely at myth. In doing so, he begins with the problem of knowing. "Human intellect is incurably abstract," Lewis says, and yet the "only realities we experience are concrete—this pain, this pleasure, this dog, this man" (65). While we interact with the man, endure the pain, or delight in the pleasure, we are never able to think about the concepts of "Pleasure, Pain

the "peninsula" of thought to the "vast continent" to which we "really belong." The use of the word "really," and the sentence that follows, where Lewis says myth is not abstract like truth nor "bound to the particular" like experience, are key to so much. Lewis finds that mere experience of the reality around us is just as limited as is thinking about reality. To experience Love here in our world is only to experience an example, an instance of it. What Lewis has been saying throughout this essay is that neither our thinking about such higher, Platonic, Ideas as Pleasure, Personality, or Pain, nor our experiencing specific instances of them is a sufficient mode of knowing. He is saying that looking along myth (rather than at it) can get us closest to the Transcendent Reality—the "vast continent we really belong to"—in which those higher ideas abide. This hierarchical concept of reality continues throughout the remainder of the essay: "myth transcends thought" and "Incarnation transcends myth." The ubiquitous pagan myth of the dying and reviving God becomes fact in the Incarnation while remaining myth. It comes down to us from a higher reality of heaven, perceived by the imagination, to factual history here on Earth. The hierarchical in Lewis's thinking about reality is clear (and will be the subject of later chapters). As Lewis goes on to talk about the story of Christ as myth become fact, which should be received by our imaginations with mythic wonder and our reason with factual certainty, he concludes that the "marriage of heaven and earth" is the coming together of "perfect myth and perfect fact" (67).

One of my favorite sentences in Lewis appears in *Perelandra*: "Long since on Mars, and more strongly since he came to Perelandra, Ransom had been perceiving that the triple distinction of truth from myth and of both from fact was purely terrestrial—was part and parcel of that unhappy division between soul and body which resulted from the Fall"

(122). In the book, Lewis imagines the Earth as fallen, and the fall not affecting worlds beyond the Earth. These places are a part of heaven. So, in heavenly worlds like Mars or Venus, knowledge might work the way it does in heaven proper: in the highest reality of heaven, there is no distinction between fact, truth, or myth. But on Earth we cannot bring fact, truth, and myth together, either in history or in our thinking except in two instances: in myth, which can give us glimpses of higher reality, and in the Incarnation, where the three came together in the person of Christ—this too, though, is a myth for us to encounter: the myth that became fact.

In summary, "Myth Became Fact" is about multiple levels of reality and how we can know them. Here on Earth, we can think *about* reality, or we can *experience* parts of it. But if we want to encounter heavenly reality, a reality not obscured by the lies and limitations on thought we face in our fallen world, we have two choices: we can get glimpses of it through myth,[3] or, as we'll see in our next example, we can wait until we get there.

The Great Divorce

Lewis also takes up the relationship between fact and truth as well as the idea of levels of reality in *The Great Divorce*, which he began writing in April 1944. Three passages are pertinent. In the first, a "white spirit" explains to an intellectual ghost that he intends to take him to see "Eternal Fact, the Father of all other facthood" (42). In the second instance,

---

3. I overview Lewis's theory of myth in my book, *The Faun's Bookshelf*. Lewis's early study of myth included Frazier's *Golden Bough*, but more influential was Barfield's *Poetic Diction: A Study in Meaning*.

the heavenly figure of George MacDonald—a nineteenth-century author whose writings, according to Lewis, baptized his imagination—explains to the Lewis persona in the book that, although hell is a state of mind, heaven is not: "Heaven is reality itself" (70). Here is a slight problem. If God is ultimate fact, then is not *he* reality itself? But if the language is figurative, then there is room for interpretation. Perhaps the true meaning of the claim "heaven is reality itself" is "All that is fully real is Heavenly" (70). Maybe *heaven* is meant as an adjective. Or, perhaps, Lewis is making a spiritual, a mystical connection between God, heaven, and reality—the idea that out of God's defining himself as the "I Am" to Moses (Exodus 3:14), we can conclude that God is Being and all other being (heaven, reality, fact) has its origins in the fullness and reality of God.

In my preface, I suggested that Lewis is more concerned about the real than he is about truth. In a profound moment in *The Great Divorce*, we see Lewis's thinking here played out in a conversation. A ghostly man who has come to the outskirts of heaven but is not yet prepared to go further in is talking to a friend he knew on Earth, a spirit who has found his way further along and taken on the fullness of the glory God intended for him. The ghost has his doubts about continuing into heaven because he insists that there must be something for him to think about and he must have "free play" of thought. He thinks that absolutes and final answers are stifling and lead to stagnation. What matters is the act of inquiry. What matters is the search for truth, not finding it. The spirit explains that the ghost believes these things because up to this point, he has experienced truth only in the abstract. He intends to take the ghost to the place where concrete Truth exists, where it can be tasted like honey and embraced like a lover (40). What Lewis is suggesting is amazing: in heaven there is no difference between truth and fact. Heaven is so thoroughly real that our ability to know about it is replaced by an ability to actually know it for what it is. On Earth, truth is just an idea—a series of ideas. In heaven, we will meet Truth face to face.

We'll return to Lewis's ideas about heaven in the last chapter.

Miracles

Miracles contains Lewis's most comprehensive approach to fact. Although not published until 1947, Lewis began writing it in 1943 and completed it in 1945. From the outset, *Miracles* doesn't seem to be as much about miracles as it is about discerning the ultimate nature of reality.

From the beginning of the book, Lewis attempts to define Nature. As noted from this and other texts previously, Lewis starts with two views, those of the Naturalist and the Supernaturalist. Of the first he says, "What the Naturalist believes is that the ultimate Fact, the thing you can't go behind, is a vast process of space and time which is *going on of its own accord*" (14). The Supernaturalist agrees "that there must be something which exists in its own right; some basic Fact" (15). However, nature is not "the whole show." The Supernaturalist believes that there are two kinds of facts: the "One Thing which is basic and original, which exists on its own," and those things that the One Thing has created. The Primary Fact exists on its own; the secondary, created facts, exist because the First exists, and their existence will end if the First fact does not maintain it (15). What follows, then, is a search for the "basic, original, self-existent Fact" (43) that is either Nature or something behind Nature.

Lewis proceeds in favor of the "something behind nature," the supernatural, which he claims to be "the most basic of all Facts" (57). He claims that "Nature is a creature, a created thing" that is falsely taken "for the ultimate self-existent Fact" (87). Then he attempts to define what the supernatural something behind Nature is. It is "an uncreated and unconditioned reality" (105). Some would say it "is not a concrete reality," that it's "not a concrete Being but 'being in general' about which nothing can be truly asserted" (115). This is unacceptable when considering that created reality is not "mere principles or generalities or theorems, but things—facts—real, resistant existences" (115). One can deduce laws from these "things"— patterns, predictions, and qualities—but they themselves are "opaque existences," that is, they possess a reality that human intelligence cannot reduce to mere abstraction. If the Something behind Nature were an abstract being in general, it could not produce concrete reality: "Book-keeping, continued to all eternity, could never produce one farthing" (116).

If anything concrete is to exist, then the "Original Thing" must be "an utterly concrete fact." God is that particular Original Thing. He is not "universal being" in the abstract, but "the Absolute Being" (116). When he proclaims, "I Am," he is "proclaiming the mystery of self-existence" (117), and when he says, "I am the Lord," he is saying he is "the ultimate Fact," and "the opaque centre of all existences, the thing that simply and entirely is, the fountain of facthood" (117). Because he so utterly and completely exists, "He can give existence away, can cause things to be, and to be really other than Himself" (118). Through the rest of Miracles, Lewis calls God "basic Fact or Actuality, the source of all other facthood" (121); "the ultimate fact . . . not an abstraction but the living God, opaque by the very fulness of His blinding actuality" (126); and "eternal self-existent Spirit, basic Fact-hood" (146).

There are, additionally, some hints in the book toward the concept of modes of reality as discussed in "Myth Became Fact" and *Mere Christianity*. But *Miracles* suggests a new mode of reality when Lewis takes up the problem of the ascension of Christ. Lewis notes those critics who say that the literalist notion that the disciples believed Christ to be flying up to a heaven in the sky sounds superstitious and primitive (*Miracles* 206). But this is to misread the disciples' perceptions. The sharp distinction modern humans make between the metaphorical and the literal did not arise until the Middle Ages and developed into its modern mode only by the seventeenth century (207; Lewis makes a similar argument in his essay "Fern-seed and Elephants"). The ancients saw heaven in the blue sky above them, but they also understood the spiritual nature of a heaven above. They didn't think of only a sky that was blue or a heaven that was abstractly spiritual (*Miracles* 207). When the disciples saw Christ ascend, the perception was for them simultaneously physical and spiritual. What they observed was both metaphorical and literal.

Thus, Lewis is saying that, in earthly reality, in human experience, there appear to be instances where metaphor and fact, the symbolic and the literal, are not as distinct as they are usually made out to be. The mode of existence that Lewis is here suggesting is one in which metaphor has concrete reality.

There are, I think, two most important takeaways from *Miracles*. Lewis wrote the book to (1) prove that Supernature is real, and (2) argue that the separation between Nature and Supernature is not as great as we think—that there is a unity in reality at all levels as proven by the central theme to Reality, the *sacramental* act of *Incarnation*, an idea to which we will return.

CHAPTER 5

Mystery and the Real

While we've already talked about knowing reality and some of the difficulties that go along with it, in this chapter we're going to look at some of Lewis's later writings on the *mystery* of the Real. Lewis scholars have suggested a change in Lewis's thinking about our ability to know the Real after the late 1940s. I'm not making that claim (in fact, I think there's a strong argument against it). What I do claim, though, is that some of Lewis's best work on the difficulties of knowing reality was written in the 1950s and 1960s. In this chapter, we'll look primarily at *The Silver Chair* (1953), *Till We Have Faces* (1956), *A Grief Observed* (1961), and *Letters to Malcolm* (1964) to see Lewis's emphasis on reality as mystery.

Knowing in Narnia

Knowledge of reality, knowledge of God—these are not easy things. This idea is expressed on an experiential level by the fourth Narnia book, *The Silver Chair*. At the beginning of the book, Eustace and Jill, two children from our world, are called into Aslan's country to perform an important task down in Narnia. They first come to Aslan's country, where they are separated because of Jill's foolish actions. This separation will complicate their quest and is the first indication of a primary problem we face in knowing the real: that we are often our own worst enemies.

In the book, Aslan's country is not Narnia; it's heaven. And in that heavenly world, thought is clearer. Aslan explains to Jill that, when she gets to Narnia, she will find the air there thick and clear thinking difficult (*Chair* 25–26). So, he gives her four signs to follow, which, if she does, will make their quest successful. Aslan is adamant about the signs: Jill must memorize them word for word, teach them to Eustace, and repeat them over and over again so that they don't forget them. The parallel between the signs and the Christian's habitual reading of scripture is clear. God's words are a guide in a world where the air is thick, and we can't always know correctly. But the key idea here is the existential relationship between knowing and acting—to act is to encounter reality in our experiences—to look along the beam more than at it. If we want to know the world as it really is, we have to *act* in the world. To fail to do so can lead to two problems: (1) it can kill us; (2) we can lose sight of what is real in the first place.

An example of the first instance—the danger of dying—occurs when Jill and Eustace, with their traveling companion Puddleglum, come to Harfang, the castle of the giants, on a cold, snowy day. A lovely lady dressed in green, who turns out to be their true enemy, has promised them warm baths and warm beds if they can get to the castle not too long after noon when the gates close (*Chair* 91). The children become focused on food and warmth and, despite Puddleglum's best attempts to redirect them, they forget about the signs. As a result, they almost die. Instead of continuing their quest, they stop at the castle, where the giants eventually intend to eat them! They only discover this fact in the nick of time and barely escape with their lives. Later, they will face one more moment where not following the signs would kill them. When Prince Rilian, the true end of their quest, calls on them to release him from the silver chair to which the Green Lady binds him for one hour each night, they are reluctant to free him. The Green Lady has told them that he is maddened and murderous during that one hour. But he asks them to free him in the name of Aslan (174). This is the last sign: that they should do whatever is asked of them in Aslan's name. At first, they are reluctant, thinking Aslan surely couldn't have meant this. They try to explain away the signs as we often do when conscience moves us to act against our desires. But then Puddleglum reminds them that Aslan did not say, "follow the signs and you'll live"; he said follow them, and that means they should do it even if they die (175). Yet, it is only by following the signs that they are saved. Rilian is set free, and they are able to escape, though not before their most terrible encounter with the *unreal*.

The Silver Chair is a book about knowledge. It asks, how can we know? How can we be sure? Ultimately what it's asking, though, is what is real? And how, then, can we know reality when we see it? The most powerful moment in the book occurs just after Rilian has been freed. At that moment, before the heroes can make their escape, the Green Lady appears and begins to cast a spell on them. The spell involves intoxicating smoke (to make the air thicker than it already is) as well as music—all meant to muddle their thinking. But the attack comes directly in terms of words, and the words express a rejection of reality. The heroes tell their host they intend to leave her realm and return to Narnia. She immediately questions the existence of such a place: Where is it? In the ceiling? What's it like? There's a sun in the sky, much like this lamp. But that must mean there is no sun, only your wish for a giant lamp. But what about Aslan? He's the true king, a lion. What's a lion? Well, it's rather like a large cat. But don't you see then, the lion, like the sun, is just something that does really exist—a cat or lamp—which you have aggrandized into an imaginary thing that doesn't exist. It's all just wish fulfillment (186–89).[1]

In the end, the only thing that saves the heroes is a choice to believe in and act on reality, despite the appearances. First, Puddleglum stamps out the witch's magic fire with his bare foot, then limping back to the others, he embraces the real:

"One word, Ma'am," he said, coming back from the fire . . ." All you've been saying is quite right, I shouldn't wonder. I'm a chap who always liked to know the worst and then put the best face I can on it . . . But there's one thing more to be said, even so. Suppose we have only dreamed, or made up, all those things—trees and grass and sun and moon and stars and Aslan himself . . . Then all I can say is that, in that case, the made-up things seem a good deal more important than the real ones. Suppose this black pit of a kingdom of yours is the only world. Well, it strikes me as a pretty poor one. And that's a funny thing, when you come to think of it. We're just babies making up a game, if you're right. But four babies playing a game can make a play-world which licks your real world hollow. That's why I'm going to stand by the play-world. I'm on Aslan's side even if there isn't any Aslan to lead it. I'm going to live as like a Narnian as I can even if there isn't any Narnia." (190–91)

1. Besides the passage here, Lewis attacks Freudian wish fulfillment in *The Pilgrim's Regress* and *Surprised by Joy*. See also his essay "Psycho-Analysis and Literary Criticism" in *Selected Literary Essays*.

Puddleglum's faith statement forces the Green Lady to reveal her *real* self—a serpent and the murderer of Rilian's mother, which then results in a physical fight (no longer a battle of words), the death of the witch, and the escape of the heroes. Reality in action saves the day.

Sometimes, however, the self-deception, which some practice, is so great that not even reality itself is enough to overcome falsehood. The dwarves in *The Last Battle* are sitting in heaven but see only a stable; they're surrounded by brilliant light but see nothing but darkness; they're given a banquet of the finest foods but taste only hay and old vegetables; and the voice of Aslan is nothing but a growl to them (181, 184). Refusing to be fooled by anyone, they choose to believe in nothing. Lewis notes at the end of *The Abolition of Man* that things cannot be explained away forever, otherwise the very ability to explain will be explained away. To see through things means to see what's really behind them. But if you go on seeing through things, you'll get to the point of not being able to see anything at all (91). In *The Great Divorce*, though Lewis says heaven is "reality itself," he claims that hell is a "state of mind" (70). The Narnian dwarves exemplify this state. Trapped in their own minds, they have rejected the Real and have made a hell of their existence.

Facing the Truth (and the Lies)

C. S. Lewis's last and least-known novel is *Till We Have Faces*. This book is hands down his most mysterious, even mystical novel, his most complex and difficult to understand. Many Lewis experts consider it his greatest work of fiction; Lewis thought so too.

In the book, Orual, the protagonist, is caught between competing views of reality. One of these views is represented by the Fox, a Greek slave brought to the kingdom of Glome by the King to become his daughters' tutor. The Fox's view of reality is the stoic view (November 20, 1962, in *Collected Letters* 3: 1382), and it is represented throughout the novel until after the Fox's death when, in the afterlife, his view radically alters. But early on, after telling Orual the story of Aphrodite and Anchises, the Fox is quick to deny the existence of such things: "Not that this ever really happened," he adds in haste (*Till We Have Faces* 8). He denies the existence of both the gods and the afterlife, saying that at death people simply go back to the dust from which they're made (17).

A second view of nature with which Orual occasionally flirts is represented in the attitude of Bardia, the captain of the palace guards and Orual's close adviser (second only to the Fox) after she becomes Queen. Though he believes in the gods, his attitude is one of avoidance: if he leaves the gods alone, perhaps they'll leave him alone (135).

The third view of reality in the novel is represented by Orual's sister Psyche. In this view the supernatural is real and benevolent. It is the view Orual eventually accepts. In the novel, Psyche is chosen as a sacrifice to the "Shadowbrute," the god of the mountain. Her only fear is that there may be no god and she will only waste away and slowly die, tied there to the tree of sacrifice. But she is determined to believe. She is convinced that "the Fox hasn't the whole truth" (70), and she is equally sure that Orual's view "that the gods are real, and viler than the vilest men" (71) is untrue. Regarding the evils the gods apparently do, Psyche says that perhaps they don't do what the priests claim they do, or perhaps, more mysteriously, they do them, but the things are not what they appear to be. And she wonders if she might indeed be about to marry a god. Notice Psyche's embrace of the mystery. But Orual will have none of it. She is convinced Psyche will be food for a beast, or worse: "I see," said Psyche in a low voice. "You think it devours the offering. I mostly think so myself. Anyway, it means death . . . And if I am to go to the god, of course it must be through death. That way, even what is strangest in the holy sayings might be true. To be eaten and to be married to the god might not be so different" (72). Life comes from death, marriage from being devoured, and no explanation is offered save that Psyche chooses to believe; she looks forward to her death with the longing of a lover (74). Her attitude makes me think of another feminine figure who was passionate for her God: Hwin the mare, who, upon meeting Aslan for the first time, said, "Please . . . you're so beautiful. You may eat me if you like. I'd sooner be eaten by you than fed by anyone else" (*The Horse and His Boy* 215).

Intending to retrieve Psyche's bones for burial after the sacrifice, Orual ascends the sacred mountain only to find her sister safe and well in the valley (the god's valley) on the other side. Psyche tells Orual the story of her lover the god, how he took her in a wind to his palace. Orual is stunned. If what Psyche has said is true, then everything Orual has believed must be swept away: Orual waivers, saying to Psyche that if it's true, then Orual has been wrong about everything her whole life. So she asks Psyche if it *is* really true (115). When Orual next pleads with Psyche to let her see her palace, Psyche is, in turn, dumbfounded, for they are in her palace and Orual cannot see it. Nor can she see fine clothing on her sister, only rags. They try to convince each other that the *reality* the other sees is false. Psyche's self-assurance is so complete that Orual almost believes her (120), but then, when Psyche mentions her lover, the god, the master of her house, Orual refuses to believe, convinced that the "whole thing must be madness" (122).

Orual spends that night in the valley but away from Psyche. The next morning, she awakens to twilight and mist. She goes to the river and kneels for a drink; when she looks up into the mist across the river, she sees the "labyrinthine beauty" in the gray of morning's light (132). She knows she must go to Psyche and ask for both her forgiveness and the god's, that is, assuming what she is witnessing is real. As she stares at the palace, doubt takes hold, and what happens next is significant. Orual wonders if what she's looking at is real. She stares at it to see if it will fade away or alter. The whole time she's watching and can still see it, she is kneeling by the water. But then she stands us, and as she does so, the palace disappears before her eyes (133). Orual immediately turns to blame: how could the gods make riddles and play games; how could they expect her to believe, in her state of distress and exhaustion, in what she *might* have seen "gazing at a mist in a half-light?" (134). She accuses the gods of mocking her and demands that if they honestly intended to lead humanity, they should do so clearly (134).

The emphasis on her position and attitude explains why her sight changes. She does not lose sight of the palace until she chooses to doubt its existence, nor does she lose sight of it until she stands. Lewis emphasizes her kneeling position to show that humility is a key to perception. The other key is faith. The significance in relation to knowing reality is in the attitude of the observer.

Orual threatens to kill herself if Psyche will not disobey her god/husband's one rule and look at his face. When Psyche does so, Orual learns the truth when his divine rage fills the valley, and in that moment the god accuses Orual of willful blindness: He presented the entire situation as being

Orual's fault—that she had known the truth all along but had used all her conversations, doubts, fears, guesses, and debates to obscure the truth she clearly knew to be the case (173). In Orual's mind, the god remakes the story to suit his anger. She makes the same accusation decades later when she hears the story of Psyche told by a priest in a distant land. Only he gets the facts wrong, saying that Psyche's sisters had seen the opulence of the palace and become jealous (243). It is at this moment that Orual decides to write her book, her accusation against the gods. She claims that they have completely changed the meaning of her actions. It was their riddle of the hidden palace and her love for Psyche that drove her actions, not vain jealousy. They forced her to guess, and she guessed wrong. If they had shown the truth clearly, she says, she would have seen. Orual completes her book, daring the gods to "answer my charge if they can" (250).

But the novel continues. Something has happened to Orual and she must tell more. Book Two of *Till We Have Faces* recounts, essentially, Orual's learning that she *is* the one who has gotten the facts wrong. It begins when she is visited by Tarin, the one-time lover of her sister Redival. He recalls Redival's loneliness, the thought of which surprises Orual. He shares Redival's confession that when they were young, Orual loved Redival, but, when the Fox came, she loved her less, and when Psyche came, Orual stopped loving Redival completely (255). Orual is shocked. It had never occurred to her to think how Redival felt when she abandoned her because Orual had always assumed that she herself was the "pitiable and ill-used one" (256).

The next shock comes when Bardia dies, and Orual learns how selfishly she had used him. Bardia's widow Ansit tells Orual that she worked him to death (261). Orual first wonders if Ansit is jealous (but how could she be jealous of so ugly a woman?) (262). But Ansit persists: "your queenship drank up his blood year by year and ate out his life" (264). She concludes that Orual is "full fed. Gorged with other men's lives, women's too: Bardia's, mine, the Fox's, your sister's—both your sisters" (265).

Shortly thereafter, Orual experiences a vision in which she sees her face in a mirror, and it is the face of Ungit, the dark goddess, mother of the Shadowbrute, she whom Orual has blamed for all her woes, especially the sacrifice of Psyche. In the vision, her father asks, "Who is Ungit?" and Orual realizes that she has been Ungit all along. Glome was a spider's web and she the eight-legged, gargantuan beast at its center, satiated and fattened on the lives of the men she claimed to love (276). Orual had been getting the facts wrong all her life, most especially the facts about her own self.

Just before this vision, however, Orual learns another fact that she had not considered before. At a ritual in the house of Ungit, Orual sees a peasant woman comforted as she prays to the goddess. That the gods might actually be good had never before occurred to her (273). She later learns, in another vision, that the goodness of the gods may itself explain the terrible, the wrathful, the extreme suffering that human beings experience in interaction with them. In the vision, Orual is trampled by gigantic golden rams, animals filled with divinity. But they do not attack her in anger: "They rushed over me in their joy . . . They butted and trampled me because their gladness led them on; the Divine Nature wounds and perhaps destroys us merely by being what it is. We call it the wrath of the gods; as if the great cataract . . . were angry with every fly it sweeps down in its green thunder" (284). And when the rams are gone, they have left Orual alive and she has come to a new understanding. For the first time, Orual learns something of the nature of the Divine, and these facts teach her more about who she really is.

She cannot completely know herself, though, until she is stripped utterly of all the facades she has hidden behind. This happens in yet another vision where she is called to accuse the gods, and, rather than read the book she has written, she pours out her innermost self. When the judge asks her, "Are you answered?" (293), she knows that the complaint *was* the answer. She knows for the first time "why the gods do not speak to us openly, nor let us answer" (294). Until all the lies have been stripped from our hearts, until the real words we mean "can be dug out of us, why should they hear the babble that we think we mean? How can they meet us face to face till we have faces?" (294). Orual finally knows who she is; she is at last ready to face the transforming and salvific accusations that the gods will make against her.

Till We Have Faces is a book about many things, but among them is the theme of seeing reality, including the reality of our own identity, for what it is. Orual, like Ransom in *Silent Planet*, must learn that she is mistaken about the facts. What she believed about nature was wrong and had to be corrected. The Divine Nature is so completely *other* that it almost destroys by its very proximity. Lewis is, furthermore, saying that self-delusion can get in the way of one's ability to know the real correctly. If we look backwards to *The Screwtape Letters*, we can see this theme similarly discussed as Uncle Screwtape constantly tells Wormwood to keep his human "patient" from ever thinking clear thoughts, not only about reality but about himself—about who *he* really is.

But to emphasize one point, Orual's critical moment of knowledge was determined by her choices and the actions that followed them. When Puddleglum chose to set Rilian free from the chair, though it might mean his own death, he came to an understanding of the real, which he could not come to in any other way. When Orual, in contrast, stood from her kneeling position, doubting the sight of the palace before her, she chose to be blind to that reality. People have wondered for centuries, "Why doesn't God just show up and prove himself to us? Why doesn't he just tell us what he wants?" The sobering answer to these questions is clear in *Till We Have Faces:* perhaps God, even now, is speaking to us. Perhaps in this very moment he is visible to those who can see and audible to those who are listening. Perhaps God isn't silent or invisible at all. Perhaps we've simply refused to hear what he has to say or see him standing right in front of us. Maybe we've blinded and deafened ourselves to him, and we've done it because we wanted to. In short, perhaps *we* are the dwarves in *The Last Battle.*

A last point: the limitation of words is a theme at the end of *Till We Have Faces.* Her encounters with the really real now ended, Orual concludes that there's nothing left to do, and all that remains is the vanity of words. She notes that her first book, her complaint against the gods, ended "with the words *no answer.* I know now, Lord, why you utter no answer. You are yourself the answer"(308). Before the absolute Real, thoughts and questions fall away. Only Being remains.[2]

Grief and Letters

A Grief Observed was written in 1960 after the death of Lewis's wife, Joy. It is a profoundly different work from *The Problem of Pain.* Whereas *Pain* had been a theological attempt to

2. Lewis's original source for the story of Cupid and Psyche is the second-century AD work of Apuleius entitled *The Golden Ass.*

make objective sense of suffering in the world at large, *Grief* is a very personal confession of one man's experience of pain, though it certainly makes profound statements about pain with which many who have suffered can identify. But its purpose and tone are clearly different from the earlier work. Three passages in *A Grief Observed* concern us most.

In the first of these, Lewis notes the difference between the conception of something outside oneself and the experience of the same: "The most precious gift that marriage gave me was this constant impact of something very close and intimate yet all the time unmistakably other, resistant—in a word, real" (30). In *Surprised by Joy* Lewis made this same distinction in relation to that experience he called Joy (219–21). There his point was that what he had been looking for inside himself was utterly and completely other, totally objective. Here he makes the same point about his wife, Joy. Every real experience of her presence always contained something more than his mental conception of who she was. This idea is not in reference to something Divine but to something human. The person of Joy, his wife, was an object before his daily perception, yet also somehow unknowable. In death, he feared, she would become even more so through the limitations of memory.

Lewis then writes about meeting a man he hadn't seen for a decade. During that time, he thought he was remembering the man accurately—his appearance, his voice, his conversation. But this memory was shattered after talking to the "real man" for just five minutes. And it wasn't that the man had changed in ten years, it was that Lewis had forgotten all those qualities that he was certain he had remembered accurately. And this makes Lewis afraid. What if what happened to his memory of the man will happen to his memory of his wife? He writes, "The rough, sharp, cleansing tang of her otherness is gone" (31–32). On the one hand, Joy was unknowable, yet on the other, her real presence would make her knowable again—more real than the images we construct out of memory. It is in the experience of the "actual presence" of a person that one really knows her (not in our trickster memories), and, at the same time, the utter otherness of that real presence makes knowing incomplete. I wonder what Lewis would have thought of virtual relationships carried out in the online world today? Would the Platonic stripping of soul from body be for him a nightmare along the lines of what was proposed by the N.I.C.E.—the deliberate disembodying of brains from bodies, of minds from flesh—in *That Hideous Strength?*

In the previous example, notice that Lewis's experience of the "real man shattered the image" Lewis had retained of him. Here *reality* is clearly a corrective. Later in *Grief* Lewis says, "All reality is iconoclastic. The earthly beloved, even in this life, incessantly triumphs over your mere idea of her. And you want her to; you want her with all her resistances, all her faults, all her unexpectedness. That is, in her foursquare and independent reality" (78). What we fail to retain in imaginative constructs, exposure to the real can correct. If knowledge is difficult, it is not necessarily impossible. But, again, Lewis looks at those moments of real knowing and says they are resistant, unexpected, and independent.

What Lewis expresses here in *A Grief Observed* is similar to something he said in *The Problem of Pain*. In reference to the story of the Incarnation, Lewis writes,

It is a story that is both like and unlike the myths of the past. "It is not transparent to the reason: we could not have invented it ourselves. It has not the suspicious *a priori* lucidity of Pantheism or of Newtonian physics. It has the seemingly arbitrary and idiosyncratic character which modern science

is slowly teaching us to put up with in this wilful universe ...
If any message from the core of reality ever were to reach us,
we should expect to find in it just that unexpectedness, that
wilful, dramatic anfractuosity which we find in the Christian faith." (*Pain* 25)

The words "resistances" and "unexpectedness" in the *Grief*
passage match the concepts of "wilfulness" and "unexpectedness" in *Pain*, and it is not too far a stretch to connect a
description of the existential realness of one person to the
realness of reality as a whole. For Lewis, the experience of
Joy's (his wife's) reality was like that of reality itself (in *Pain*)
or the ecstatic experience (which he called Joy) that calls to
humankind through the real (in *Surprised by Joy*).

I'm returning to this much earlier book (*The Problem of
Pain*) in the Lewis corpus for two reasons. The first is to
show, as I briefly mentioned at the beginning of this chapter,
that Lewis's ideas about the nature of the real and our ability to know it are more consistent than some Lewis experts
have previously thought. *Pain* and *Grief* approach pain in
different ways, the earlier book looking more *at* it, the latter
looking more *along* it. But there is a unity in Lewis's postcon-
version thought that is easy to miss, and in some instances,
this unity of thought can be seen prior to his conversion,
which brings me to my second reason for recalling *The Problem of Pain* here. It is the point made in *Grief* that "reality is
iconoclastic" (78). In a recent study of Lewis's preconversion
narrative poem, *Dymer*, Jerry Root argues that this theme of
iconoclasm is present in this very early poem and throughout
Lewis's works (see Root's *Splendour in the Dark*). The idea is
a simple one: whatever we think we know about reality—
about God, about the facts of Nature, about the people in
our lives, even about ourselves (as *Till We Have Faces* makes

clear)—we are, to some extent, wrong. And the cure for our bad thinking about the real is reality itself. In encounters with reality, our false ideas and images are shattered. Here is the surest connection between reality and truth: the real regularly tears down what we think to be true, forcing us either to reject it or to pursue true truth—that is, truth that is *really true*—all our lives. This, again, is an idea emphasized in Lewis's later works but also present in his earlier ones.

And it is certainly a central theme in *Letters to Malcolm* to which we now turn. In letter 15, Lewis considers the relationship between himself as subject and the reality he sees around him as object. In prayer, this relationship becomes utterly real to him because he knows that God is the root existence for both himself and his environment (79). Indeed, it is by seeing (iconoclastically) that these things—his image of his self and his conception of the created reality that is open to his perceptions—are not "ultimate realities" that he is able to believe in them as realities at all (80). The idea is that if God is Ultimate Reality, then the facades the finite perceiver takes as reality can be more confidently believed in. The key to this paradox is in the reality of the delusion. Lies and dreams present false reality but, once they are known for what they are, only their ability to deceive ceases. They remain real lies and real dreams: "In fact we should never ask of anything 'Is it real?,' for everything is *real*. The proper question is 'A real what?,' e.g., a real snake or real *delirium tremens?*" (80). Lewis expressed this same idea in the late 1930s in a book he coauthored called *The Personal Heresy*: "everything that is real is a real something, although it may not be what it pretends to be. 'What pretends to be a crocodile may be a (real) dream; what pretends at the breakfast-table to be a dream may be a (real) lie'" (109n). The objects around us or even our own conception of the human self will be lies if taken at face value.

But if they are taken as real creations of a higher Reality that gives roots and a form, then they can meet one another genuinely. We can believe in the reality of our own selves, the reality of the objects around us, and the reality of our encounter with them. Created matter and created mind meet one another as "the end-products of divine activity" (80). Or put it this way: two people meet each other, get to know each other, fall in love, and get married. After a year of living together, they realize they didn't know a thing about each other. But when can we ever know anything about other people? It's the same problem with our senses: how do I know I'm not dreaming? How do I know what clothes to pick out when everyone around me says I'm color-blind (and how do I know they're right)? How do I know I'm really seeing a creature swimming along the surface of Loch Ness? How do I know I'm not living in a Matrix created by machines to keep me under control in a virtual reality? Lewis's answer is that God gives us our real existence and anchors us to a real Nature that he created. I'm a real person—God says so. I'm writing a book. What appears to be paper on a screen is just an electronic series of ones and zeros, true, but they are real ones and zeros that have been shaped into a real language that makes it possible for me to write real words on a real page, though the page is not made of paper. When this book is done, I'm going to send it to a real publisher—people whom I have never met who nevertheless respond to my emails or talk to me on the phone in ways that make sense to my belief that they are really there. Eventually, computers may get good enough to mimic these people, and I won't know the difference, but the computers will still be real because they are part of a real creation, or Nature. The publisher may not publish my book. But if they do, the book will be read by real people (many of whom I'll never meet) or by no one depending on the caprices of the American book

market—which is to say, the book buying and reading habits of real people (and, of course, if you're reading this right
now, I appear to have been successful in the steps listed in this
example). I don't know these people (who may get to know
me a little through my book or not at all by *not* reading it),
but I know they're real—God says so. His self-existent, basic,
Facthood gives facthood to me, other people, and the world of
nature in which we live. Nevertheless, we can be wrong about
what we believe about nature (such as my belief that this book
will sell in the millions or my belief that animals can talk; they
just choose not to), and though the nature we live in is real,
there is a Reality behind nature, a Divine activity that makes it
possible for us who live in nature to encounter each other with
the faith that much of what we are experiencing of nature and
each other is real.

Lewis believes "that this 'real world' and 'real self' are very
far from being rock-bottom realities" (81), and here he brings
to culmination an idea that he has expressed for decades. We
have seen previously his idea that God is the Ultimate Fact
from Whom all other facthood flows; his idea of God as the
most concrete of all realities; and his constant claim that reality is difficult and complex, that there is much that surprises
people and is difficult to understand. Nowhere is this truer
than in our understanding of God. Lewis speaks of his frus-
tration with knowing both himself and the God to whom
he is praying in chapter 15 of *Letters to Malcolm*. Lewis says
that in the midst of prayer, he realizes that the "real world"
and "real self" aren't "rockbottom realities." In prayer Lewis
pictures himself as an actor on a stage that he cannot leave.
At the same time, however, he realizes that the actor is a real
person who *does* have a real life beyond the stage. And the real
person in his life outside the stage is trying to speak from his
real self (not his acting self) to someone other than the other

actors. He is trying to pray. And the prayer he prays first is, "May it be the real I who speaks. May it be the real Thou that I speak to" In prayer, God works as an "iconoclast. Every idea of Him we form, He must in mercy shatter. The most blessed result of prayer would be to rise thinking, 'But I never knew before. I never dreamed'" (81–82).

But what is true of our knowledge of God is even true of our knowledge of nature. In Lewis's day, limitations on our ability to know fact became increasingly clear in science through advances in physics. Lewis notes that the set on a stage, for example, does indeed have existence, but to take a hammer and chisel to the stage house will not produce pieces of brick but a hole in the canvas. In the same way, if we study the essence of material reality, we won't find what our imaginations have always thought it to be. We will only "get mathematics" (*Malcolm* 80). In his 1943 essay "Dogma and the Universe," Lewis writes, "As regards material reality, we are now being forced to the conclusion that we know nothing about it save its mathematics" (125). And, again, in *The Problem of Pain* where Lewis tells us that science in his day was saying that quantum physics meant the physical universe could not be pictured, and any attempt to do so would move us further from reality, not closer to it (86).

Throughout his writings Lewis borrows from contemporary scientific thinking about the real to demonstrate that there are limitations to knowing it rightly. This becomes common sense when one considers that Lewis wrote many of his own books as correctives. The purpose behind his apologetics and, to an extent, his fiction as well, was to correct people's wrong ideas (and images) about reality. It was to be iconoclastic. No such works would be needed if reality were not difficult to grasp. Reality itself must constantly correct our perceptions—whether rational abstractions or imaginative visions—of reality itself. But we can accept that reality because there is a higher Reality, an utterly objective God whose own action gives rise and objectivity to all created reality, including ourselves.

Reality is a mystery. It breaks in on us, blowing up and tearing down our false views and sometimes our most cherished beliefs. It corrects our faltered memories. It tells us when we're lying to ourselves (often despite our best efforts to refuse to listen to what it's telling us). It uses facts to tell us we're missing the facts, that is, we're missing the reality behind the facts that lets us truly know that it *is* possible for us to know truly. And reality offers us a strange paradox: the truth that, if we want to know God, the Higher Reality behind all reality, we will first come short, but then we may come to realize this failure through our encounters with reality, which, as Lewis says, is iconoclastic. Lewis is teaching us that reality simultaneously teaches us about God (and ourselves) and fails to teach us about God; however, it can help correct everything we falsely believe.

CHAPTER 6

Hierarchy Part One

Levels and Kinds of Reality

Up and Down, Side to Side, and Inside Out

In this chapter we'll explore Lewis's conception of multiple *levels* of *reality* more fully. In the essay "De Futilitate," Lewis makes clear that there are only three ways to view the universe: (1) the view of the scientist; (2) the view of the Western Idealist and Oriental Pantheist; and (3) the view of Jews, Muslims, and Christians. Lewis rejects the first view because it does not account for all the facts, and he rejects the second view because it reduces reality to something "not quite real." Lewis abandoned his own brand of idealism (which saw spirit as good and matter as evil) when he became a theist, thus adopting the third view, "that though Nature is real as far as she goes, still there are other realities" ("De Futilitate" 671).

Lewis's view of reality is at least partially hierarchical or, as he says in *Miracles*, "monarchical" (15), having something above and something below. Lewis moves quickly away from any flattened naturalist view of reality, whether in his argument of the Moral Law or Law of Nature in *Mere Christianity* or in his natural versus supernatural dichotomy in *Miracles*. Lewis is very clear in stating that Nature is not God (*Reflections on the Psalms* 67), that God created Nature and is Master over it (*Miracles* 87), that God is outside Nature (*Mere Christianity* 44), that Nature derives from God (*Miracles* 15), and that God is the "fountain of facthood" (117) and the "source of all other facthood" (121). He also says that Nature is temporary: "Nature is mortal; we shall outlive her" ("Weight of Glory" 17).

Hierarchy is not just a division between God and Nature. Though Lewis begins with two levels, he does not stop there. In her book *Real Presence*, Leann Payne argues that Lewis distinguished physical created Nature from immaterial created Supernature and both from the uncreated Absolute Reality—God—above all Natures (44). Furthermore, Lewis thinks that there "may be Natures piled upon Natures, each supernatural to the one beneath it" until we attain the heights of God's realm of "pure spirit," where even then, in the presence of God, we may be closer to all of these Natures in some "more dynamic presence on all levels" ("Miracles" 10).

Going even beyond this, Lewis explores the idea of more than just a hierarchy of vertical realities in his writings. In two places he talks about the possibility of side-by-side realities, what physicists and lovers of science fiction today call the multiverse. We learn that Narnia, for example, is not in our universe at all. It's in a completely separate universe where time runs differently than it does in ours. In *The Magician's Nephew*, Digory and Polly discover a "Wood Between the Worlds" that has numerous pools in it, and each pool at least appears to lead to completely different universes (31–44). And in his unfinished sequel to *Out of the Silent Planet*, a fragment published as *The Dark Tower*, Lewis tells the story of a universe parallel to ours where many things are similar and many things different in the most sinister ways (*The Dark Tower and Other Stories* 15–91). So, in addition to vertical realities, Lewis posits the possibility of horizontal ones. There may be natures piled *on* natures, but there may also be natures stacked *beside* natures. Yet even this isn't all.

In *The Discarded Image*, Lewis describes the way Medieval thinkers envisioned the real. One of the falsehoods about Medieval people was that they thought the world was at the center of the universe, thus showing how important the world and humanity were in God's creation. Lewis says this is not true. While they did believe that the Earth was at the center of a *physical* universe, Medieval thinkers also believed that it was, somehow, at the farthest edge of *spiritual* reality. When seen with human eyes, the Earth seemed to be at the center of things. But when seen with spiritual eyes, an inversion made the world the farthest from the center. They did not think of themselves as the most important beings in creation but as the least important (116, 119). This idea is echoed in *The Last Battle*, where the heroes of Narnia find that, as they go "further up and further in" to Narnia, they discover that inside a garden high up in that world, there is a whole new Narnia, larger on the inside than it is on the outside. Within each Narnia, there is a whole other Narnia, but that Narnia (though within) is somehow larger than the Narnia that surrounds it (224–25). Narnia within Narnia, reality within reality. And each reality is hierarchically more real, somehow larger than the ones without. So, Lewis imagines the possibility of vertical, horizontal, and even interior realities, a multiverse of being that is even more than merely hierarchical. Like a cube, it may have vertical realities, horizontal realities, and realities of depth.

Ought as Is

As we saw in *Mere Christianity*, Lewis details an aspect of his hierarchical view of reality, which he only touches on in other works. Though he refers to Natural Law elsewhere, in

Mere Christianity Lewis not only distinguishes what people do from what they ought to do but suggests that the "ought" is its own kind of reality. I want to summarize and then expand on this idea. The argument Lewis follows in *Mere Christianity* begins with proving two facts: (1) humanity has a universal sense of right and wrong, and (2) human beings cannot live up to such values (7). Next, he distinguishes between the laws of Nature and the Law of Human Nature, noting that the former are not laws at all, only descriptions, whereas the latter are prescriptions that define how people ought to behave (as opposed to how they actually behave) (14–16). What follows is the conclusion of multiple realities: the Moral Law has to be, in some way, a reality—something that is actually there—not something we have invented. But it's not a fact in the way we normally thing about fact—it's not a fact in the way our actions are facts. Instead, Lewis says, we have to come to the realization "that there is more than one kind of reality" (16–17). Lewis argues that there is reality that can be described—the reality of the fact, the event, the moment in history. But there is another kind of reality, too: a completely "other" reality, rule, or law that tells people how they ought to behave. We saw in *Abolition of Man* that Lewis refers to this as the *Tao*. Now to carry it further.

In "The Poison of Subjectivism" Lewis takes up the relationship between God and this other kind of reality, Moral Law. According to Lewis, one's first inclination toward the relationship—to say that God is the author of Morality—is an insufficient response. The Moral Law consists of "fundamental imperatives" that are "absolute and categorical" ("Poison" 663). They deserve humans' "absolute allegiance," as does God. This, however, raises a difficult dilemma: "Are these things right because God commands them or does God command them because they are right?" (663). If the former is true, then God could make whatever rules he wanted and, as such, he would be "emptied of meaning," possessing in his Infinite Nature only one infinite quality: absolute power to do whatever he wanted. In this scenario, "the commands of an omnipotent fiend would have the same claim on us as those of the 'righteous Lord'" (663). If the other option is true, however, God becomes a cosmic cop who must execute a Moral Law that is separate from and comes before him. In other words, if God invents morality, he's just a cosmic bully, telling us what's right and wrong because he's got the power to do so. But if Moral Truth exists apart from God, he has to answer to it as a higher power, the way a police officer answers to the Constitution. Neither option is acceptable.

Lewis's solution involves the Trinity, an only slightly imaginable existence that transcends the idea of personhood understood by humanity. If the Personhood of God transcends human comprehension, then perhaps "the duality which seems to force itself upon us when we think, first, of our Father in Heaven, and, secondly, of the self-evident imperatives of the moral law, is not a mere error but a real (though inadequate and creaturely) perception of things that would necessarily be two in any mode of being which enters our experience, but which are not so divided in the absolute being of the superpersonal God" ("Poison" 664). When we think of a law in conjunction with thinking about a person, we can think of the person writing the law or obeying the law. And when we think of the person writing the law, we think of him or her doing it according to some higher pattern of morality, which means the person is not really the author of the law, or we think of the person as just making up the law "arbitrarily" according to his or her own desires in which case the law loses any sense of goodness we would feel compelled to follow. Lewis concludes that one's best response is two negations: "that God neither *obeys* nor *creates* the moral law." Thus, "the good is uncreated" (80). It is clear, then, that "God is not merely good, but Goodness; *Goodness* is not merely divine, but God" (80). So, in the Nature of God there is a single and Absolute Reality that in our fallen world is perceived as separate realities: that reality that *describes* (here is what *is*) and that reality that *prescribes* (here is what *ought* to be).

Throughout his works, Lewis recognizes a hierarchy of Being based in Moral goodness. The greater the good in a thing, the more real it is. Conversely, "evil is not a real *thing* at all, like God. It is simply good *spoiled*. That is why I say there can be good without evil, but no evil without good . . . Evil is a parasite. It is there only because good is there for it to spoil and confuse" (September 12, 1933, in *Collected Letters* 2: 122). Lewis envisions a vast chain of being or "ontological continuity" from the Absolute Goodness that is God down to the absolute worst reprobate or devil (*Letters to Malcolm* 69). At the lowest end of this hierarchy of Moral Being is hell. In *The Problem of Pain*, Lewis describes hell as the "the outer rim where being fades away into nonentity" (127). In *The Great Divorce*, the Lewis-narrator is taught that hell is smaller than one pebble on earth and smaller than one atom of heaven (138).

There is a popular statement about good and evil that goes, "You can't have good without evil." C. S. Lewis disagrees. The promise of heaven is a promise of the death of evil. The promise of a God who loves is a promise that God did not create evil and does not intend to see it continue. Evil cannot exist without Good because evil is a parasite that lives by twisting goodness. This means evil can be destroyed, ended, finished, and heaven can be paradise forever and God's victory final and complete—in us and in the whole of creation. If this doesn't seem possible, if we can't imagine a world without evil, it is either because we lack imagination or don't know what good really is—we've never really seen it before, never experienced it in reality. Or if we did, we shied away from it. Consider those people whom we all know who are so holy, loving, and giving that they at once attracted our attention, even our desire to be around them, while they also make us feel uncomfortable, guilty, and ashamed as we compare ourselves to them. That's the problem we face. We can't imagine perfect goodness because we ourselves are tainted by evil. Good came into the world once, and we missed him completely; we even crucified him.

CHAPTER 7

Hierarchy Part Two

Lewis and Plato

We cannot discuss levels of reality in Lewis's writings without talking about Lewis and Plato. Some of the passages we've encountered offer glimpses of a Platonic bent in Lewis's thinking. Recall how the characters in *The Great Divorce* are ghostly apparitions in the density of heaven, and that hell has no more being than a pebble even on Earth. Recall also the "ontological continuity" that exists between God at the heights of *Being* and the lowliest sinner here on Earth (*Malcolm* 69). In exploring Lewis's idea of Moral Being and levels of reality, we clearly saw a hierarchy based on good and evil. The idea of Platonic hierarchy, however, is not quite the same thing, and in short, at times Lewis agrees with Plato, and at times he does not.

For example, Lewis clearly distinguishes between Platonism and Christianity when he writes, "The essential attitude of Platonism is aspiration or longing: the human soul, imprisoned in the shadowy, unreal world of Nature, stretches out its hands and struggles towards the beauty and reality of that which lies (as Plato says) 'on the other side of existence' ... In Christianity, however, the human soul is not the seeker but the sought: it is God who seeks, who descends from the outer world to find and heal Man" ("Edmund Spenser 1552–99"

144). While Plato's idea of longing is something we have seen in Lewis, Plato believed that material reality was less real than the reality of pure ideas and unchanging forms; therefore, if we want to know truth, we must aspire to that higher realm.[1] But in a letter to Arthur Greeves, Lewis notes that the Christian story is the "true myth" by which God reveals himself to us: "The 'doctrines' we get *out of* the true myth are of course *less* true: they are translations into our *concepts* and *ideas* of that wh[ich] God has already expressed in a language more adequate, namely the actual incarnation, crucifixion, and resurrection" (October 18, 1931, in *Collected Letters* 1: 977). In other words, the reality of Jesus in the material world is truer than any truth statements made about him. Here Lewis seems to completely invert the Platonic model in relation to the coming of God into the material world. The mutable form of Christ on Earth was more real than that Platonic world of immutable forms, truer than the pure ideas. When God becomes human, he does not cease to be God. If God is the most real "thing" there is, he is still so when he takes on a physical body. Perhaps Lewis is redefining Plato here, or perhaps he is reading Plato as he was meant to be read, or, again, perhaps Lewis is revealing the fulfillment (in Christ) of what Plato only hinted at.

In another letter to Greeves, Lewis writes, "I agree that we don't know what a spiritual body is. But I don't like *contrasting* it with (your words) 'an actual, physical body'. This suggests that the spiritual body wd. be the opposite of 'actual'—i.e. some kind of vision or imagination . . . I suspect the distinction is the other way round—that it is something compared with which our present bodies are half real and phantasmal" (August 19, 1947, in *Collected Letters* 3: 1573–74). The present

1. See especially Plato's famous Allegory of the Cave in book 7 of *The Republic.*

human body is a shadow of the true form that awaits. Nevertheless, Lewis found value in the physical body and thought Plato did not, as a letter to Dom Bede Griffiths indicates: "But I fear Plato thought the concrete flesh and grass bad, and have no doubt he was wrong" (January 17, 1940, in *Letters of C. S. Lewis* 335). In the above letter to Greeves we see a hint of the metaphor Lewis uses in *The Great Divorce*, where he makes heaven a physically dense, hard place, a metaphor that appears again in *Miracles* in the description of God as the most concrete reality there is. Lewis associates higher reality with a more concrete materiality for the sake of human imagination—so that we can *see* that it is a mistake to think of spiritual things as less real than physical things. Spirit is often associated with wind (in the Greek New Testament, they are the same word). We think of wind as light and airy and something we pass through . . . that is until a hurricane hits. Then we see the whirlwind. Then we learn how concrete "spirit" can be.

This metaphorical connection between higher reality and increasingly solid materiality helps further explain the puzzling description in "Myth Became Fact" of Myth as the "father of innumerable truths on the abstract level . . . the mountain whence all the different streams arise which become truths down here in the valley of separation, *in hac valle abstractionis*" (66), a passage we've considered before. The "valley of separation" here is the valley of abstraction—truth is separated from concrete myth when it comes down to the human world; here it can only be perceived as abstraction.[2] Lewis associates myth with heaven in this essay. And so when he

2. A wonderful fictional exception to this rule occurs in a novel by Lewis's fellow Inkling, Charles Williams. In *The Place of the Lion*, the Transcendent Ideas descend to Earth and wreak havoc in the world of particulars.

says myth is not abstract like truth nor bound to the particular like experience, he is arguing a heaven of Platonic forms. In heaven, ideas aren't concepts, they're things. On Earth our thoughts are about the things, or our experiences are just partial examples of the things. Here below we can receive them only as tastes (shadows) or ideas of the concrete forms that exist above. This returns us to Lewis's vision of heaven in *The Great Divorce*. In the conversation between one heavenly person and his old friend the intellectual apostate, the ghostly man argues that to find the answers to all questions would be stifling and lead to stagnation. His concrete counterpart replies that his friend believes this because he's only known truth in the abstract, but in heaven he'll meet Truth in person (40). On Earth, truth is abstract statements one makes about reality. In heaven, truth is concretely real.

So, in "Myth Became Fact" we are given the image of a heavenly mountain, the world of myth, which is both universal and concrete. Born from this world of myth are streams that flow like rivers, losing their concretion, their solidity, and entering the mind here in the "valley of separation" as abstractions, truths. Our world of abstraction, however, is also the world of materiality, where experience is concrete but bound to the particular. And, most paradoxically, this world of the material is only shadows, suggests Lewis. This mingling in Lewis of concrete and abstract as paradoxical, almost contradictory, metaphors helps illuminate his definition of allegory, which, in turn, helps the reader make more sense of his vision of the hierarchical real.

In *The Allegory of Love*, Lewis writes, "It is of the very nature of thought and language to represent what is immaterial in picturable terms. What is good or happy has always been high like the heavens and bright like the sun" (44). In the next paragraph Lewis says that this "fundamental equivalence between the immaterial and the material may be used by the mind in two ways." In the first way, one uses images to express thoughts and feelings. Thus, if one is torn between anger and gentleness, he might explain his "state of mind by inventing a person called *Ira* with a torch and letting her contend with another invented person called *Patientia*" (45). To do this is to make *allegory*. But there is another way to use the relationship between the material and the immaterial: "If our passions, being immaterial, can be copied by material inventions, then it is possible that our material world in its turn is the copy of an invisible world. As the god Amor and his figurative garden are to the actual passions of men, so perhaps we ourselves and our 'real' world are to something else. The attempt to read that something else through its sensible imitations, to see the archetype in the copy, is what I mean by symbolism or sacramentalism" (45). We'll come back to sacramentalism, but immediately important in this passage is the way in which Lewis deals with the material versus the immaterial. In *Allegory*, there are invisible ideas that people describe in images; these images mimic a more concrete visible reality, which may itself be only an imitation of a higher invisible reality.[3] This passage connects us back to Lewis's description of the medieval cosmos, which, though it placed the Earth at the center of the physical universe, it reversed the position spiritually, placing the Earth on the outer rim, "the outside edge where being fades away on the border of nonentity" (*The Discarded Image* 116).

In the last of the Narnia books, *The Last Battle*, we are presented with the possibility of multiple realities described in Lewis's most overtly Platonic writing. The heroes enter a new Narnia, which turns out to be "More like the real thing"

3. For Lewis, allegory reached its apex in the works of Edmund Spenser, especially *The Faerie Queene*, which Lewis read several times.

(210). We learn that the old Narnia, the only one ever known in the books, "was not the real Narnia. That had a beginning and an end. It was only a shadow or a copy of the real Narnia . . . just as our own world, England and all, is only a shadow or copy of something in Aslan's real world" (211–12). Digory says it is as different as a real thing is from a shadow or as waking is from a dream. Then he makes the important statement: "It's all in Plato, all in Plato" (212). At this point the narrator takes over and tries to explain how the new Narnia was different from—better than—the old one by asking us to recall a time when we might have been in a room that looked out on a beautiful land or seascape. We stand at the window, gazing at the beauty beyond. Then we turn. On the opposite wall from the window is a mirror, and we catch sight of the landscape or seascape in the mirror just for a moment. And there we see the same thing we've just seen, but somehow the reflection in the mirror is "different—deeper, more wonderful, more like places in a story: in a story you have never heard but very much want to know. The new [Narnia] was a deeper country: every rock and flower and blade of grass looked as if it meant more" (212–13). The most important part of the passage is this last line. The significance of the new Narnia is not its physical size but the largeness of its Being. And as being increases, so does *meaning*. The unicorn, Jewel, summarizes the impression everyone is experiencing: "I have come home at last! This is my real country!" (213). Lewis's vision to this point in *The Last Battle* is clearly Platonic, similar to that which he shows us in *The Great Divorce*. But, par for Lewis, the vision becomes more complex as hierarchy is combined with interiority.

As we saw in the last chapter, when they reach the golden gates of the garden at the center of the new Narnia, the heroes enter, only to find that "the place was far larger than it had seemed from the outside" (222). Notes Mr. Tumnus, "The further up and further in you go, the bigger everything gets. The inside is larger than the outside." Lucy looks at the garden in the new Narnia and realizes it is not a garden but a whole world, one she immediately recognizes: "'This is still Narnia,['" she says, "'] and more real and more beautiful than the Narnia down below, just as *it* was more real and more beautiful than the Narnia outside the stable door! I see . . . world within world, Narnia within Narnia'" (224–25). Lewis's hierarchy expands, going beyond the image of vertical levels. Here the higher beings/realities are not above as much as they are within the lower, yet not within for they are larger.

Finally, there is another complex image, multiple realities on a plane that is both hierarchical and horizontal. There is a great "chain of mountains which ringed round the whole world" (225). Aslan's country is there. And out from "the great mountains of Aslan" jut spurs of lesser mountains—these are the "*real* countries," the most real Narnia and the real England, which join together as the heroes journey further up and further in (226). Numerous real worlds must jut out from these mountains, and from them the numerous shadow worlds. Here there is hierarchy, horizontality, and interiority. The journey to heaven is both upward and inward but may involve excursions around the rim. If Lewis does move beyond Plato here, it is, nevertheless, with the recognition of Platonic conception overall. This is seen at the end of *The Last Battle* when Aslan refers to their old worlds as "Shadowlands" (228).

Does knowing something about Lewis's views on Plato really matter in the grand scheme of things? If nothing else, it reminds us that *things* are a grand scheme. Reality is complicated, more complex than we tend to think it is. And as such it might be good to practice some humility when talking about or acting on what we know (or think we know) about it. If reality is hierarchical, horizontal, multiple, and interior all at the same time, we're dealing with something bigger than we are. The ant's mistake in following the crumbs into my house is in his failure to realize that larger things exist, and they have giant cans of Raid on standby.

In addition, these chapters on hierarchy remind us that most of reality is invisible to us. Even parts of physical reality are things we can't see (like X-rays and microbes). There's so much more to the real than our senses can discover. And so we must turn to our thoughts and ultimately our faith, which allows us to see what we cannot. A bad idea arose in the last hundred years or so that faith is the enemy of reason.[4] The Bible, Lewis reminds us, tells us something else. It tells us that faith is the enemy of sight (II Corinthians 5:7). Lewis gets to the heart of the matter in his essay, *Religion: Reality or Substitute:*

> There are things, say in learning to swim or to climb, which look dangerous and aren't. Your instructor tells you it's safe. You have good reason from past experience to trust him. Perhaps you can even see for yourself, by your own reason, that it is safe. But the crucial question is, will you be able to go on believing this when you actually see the cliff edge below you or actually feel yourself unsupported in the water? You will have no rational grounds for disbelieving. It is your senses and your imagination that are going to attack belief. Here, as in the New Testament, the conflict is not between faith and reason but between faith and sight. We can face things which we know to be dangerous if they don't look or sound too dangerous; our real trouble is often with things we

4. Perhaps beginning with Kierkegaard's "leap of faith" but certainly influenced by the rise of science-as-epistemological authority.

know to be safe but which look dreadful. Our faith in Christ wavers not so much when real arguments come against it as when it looks improbable—when the whole world takes on that desolate look which really tells us much more about the state of our passions and even our digestion than about reality. ("Religion: Reality or Substitute" 42–43)

Though this passage sidetracks us a little bit, the main point is a good one, and it helps me make a different point about reality: If we don't approach it with faith, we'll be blind to the majority of what's actually there. We'll be Oedipus before blind Tereisias (the only one of the two who could see), Neo in the *Matrix* never taking the red pill, the dwarfs at the end of *The Last Battle* who couldn't even see that they were in heaven.

CHAPTER 8

Transposition

Look at this sentence from *Miracles:* "If we must have a mental picture to symbolise Spirit, we should represent it as something *heavier* than matter" (123). Within the context of its passage, the statement is clear. But taken by itself, its tone (in the words, "if we must") suggests that we should shy away from mental or imaginative pictures of Spirit. Are our images of heaven false? Are the symbols, the metaphors we use to describe higher levels of reality, misleading to the point that they hinder rather than aid understanding? The response Lewis makes in his theory of Transposition is, in part, to suggest that the symbolic may be more real, that is, more literal than we think.

Lewis suggests this idea when he refers in "The Weight of Glory" to Nature as a "first sketch" (17). "Nature is only the image, the symbol" of a greater glory to which humankind is called. Ultimately, people "are summoned to pass in through Nature, beyond her, into that splendour which she fitfully reflects." The idea of reflection is key. Throughout his writing Lewis finds reality in metaphor—moments of the literal in figural fragments. A favorite example is in regard to marriage and sexuality: Marriage in Christian thinking is centered in the words of Christ when he said that a husband and wife are a single creature, a single body. "Christians believe that when He said this He was not expressing a sentiment but stating a fact" (*Mere Christianity* 88). In *Miracles*, sexuality is related specifically to the concept of transposition: "Even our sexuality should be regarded as the transposition into a minor key of that creative joy which in Him is unceasing and irresistable" (121).

Another favorite association for Lewis is between Transposition and the Incarnation. The first significant miracle, according to Lewis, is humanity itself. How is it possible that spirit indwells a physical body? This indwelling is almost as miraculous as the Incarnation, where the "Divine Spirit dwelled within the created and human spirit of Jesus" (*Miracles* 147), and it is significant transpositionally, that is, as a sign that even our dual existence as spirit and flesh is not a strange exception but a partial image of Christ's Incarnation—that we represent the minor version of the major key. Lewis sees in the comparison a grand scheme or unifying principle in which God descends into human spirit, human spirit into nature, thoughts into senses and emotions, adult minds into sympathy with children, people into sympathy with animals; and, if this is so, "then everything hangs together and the total reality, both Natural and Supernatural, in which we are living is more multifariously and subtly harmonious than we had expected" (147). In this Lewis says we glimpse a "new key principle": the ability of all things "Higher" to descend, the ability of the "greater to include the less" (147). This is Transposition.

This descending occurs in the Incarnation, but the pattern is not one of singular direction. God descends in order to reascend and raise the broken creation along with him (148). And this pattern in the action of Divine Nature is visible in all of Nature herself: in the reproduction of plant life from a seed, in the birth of animals from the hidden interior of the womb. Lewis calls this pattern of Descent and Reascent "the very formula of reality" (166), from the heights of living being to the depths of death itself. The "very pattern of reality" is in Christ, who truly lives and so can truly die (172): Since the transcendent above can come down to what is below, Christ who has from time and beyond time surrendered himself to God the Father—who has essentially died to himself through all eternity—is best suited to descend into physical death.

From the transpositional view of reality, we can glean an interconnectedness that we have only glimpsed so far. Transposition certainly suggests the idea of hierarchy in Lewis's view of the real. The pattern of descent and reascent works in a vertical relationship. Because God is above, he is able to descend to us who are below. However, the purpose of descent is to take up the lower into the higher. Humanity is raised up as he is made low. Does this mean that hierarchy exists now because of the fall, but will later disappear? No. Lewis says that Christ's humbling himself before the Father and subsequent glorification by him is an eternal action, and this pattern is ultimately the model of all creation.

Of course, Lewis's magnum opus on *Transposition* is his sermon of that title. He begins with a problem: how can one know whether the instances of speaking in tongues or glossolalia that have been exhibited throughout the centuries in church history are legitimate spiritual miracles or simple human hysteria? ("Transposition" 9–20). From here Lewis raises the larger problem behind the specific instance. All that people do that has traditionally been associated with the supernatural seems, from the skeptic's point of view, to have natural roots. He cites as example the great religious mystics whose language of experiencing the Divine is the same as what we use in describing erotic experiences (10). All that we label *supernatural* in our experiences can be explained by natural means.

To answer the skeptic, Lewis asks if there is any example in Nature of a higher thing reaching down to a lower. If such an example can be found, insights may arise as to the way Supernature operates (11). He suggests looking at the experience of aesthetic rapture and notes that the emotional response is frequently accompanied by a physical response, as if the emotional intensity spills over into the body. Then he notices that the physical response to extreme delight is not too far different from the same physical response people experience in anguish. We may weep at both; we may feel a knot in the stomach with both. Yet the emotions themselves are opposites. That the emotional life is richer, more varied than the life of the sensations is proven in that the body's responses to various experiences are fewer than human emotional responses. The body must use the same physical responses for a larger variety of emotional responses. It cries in pain, and it cries in Joy. This indicates the higher coming down into the lower—that example Lewis is looking for (13). The poorer can never have one-to-one correspondence with the richer.

Lewis's second observation is that the word *symbolism* is not always a sufficient label for the relationship between the higher medium and its transposition into the lower. Symbolism works perfectly for some cases such as "the relationship between speech and writing" where written words exist "solely for the eye" and spoken words for the ear (15). The distinction between the sign and what it signifies is complete and clear. In pictures, however, there is a mixing of sign and signified. For example, "The suns and lamps in pictures seem to shine only because real suns or lamps shine on them; that is, they seem to shine a great deal because they really shine a little in reflecting their archetypes. The sunlight ... is a sign, but also something more than a sign, and only a sign because it is also more than a sign, because in it the thing signified is really in a certain mode present. If I had to name the relation I should call it not symbolical but sacramental" (15). Lewis's point: some instances of symbolism are purely representational. Others are transpositional or sacramental: the thing being symbolized is somehow *actually* present in the symbol itself.

"Transposition" continues with a summary of the concept: "Transposition occurs wherever the higher reproduces itself in the lower" (16). Consider as an example the relationship between mind and brain. Seen from below, the brain is all there is, and thought is simply the movement of atoms. But that movement corresponds to numerous varied activities of mind, fitting the model of transposition.

Lewis next returns to the problem of Spirit and Nature (16). Remember from his introduction that what may be an event engendered by spirit nevertheless appears to be only a natural phenomenon. His response now is that, in transposition, this is the way it should look. Materialists will only see religious hysteria in glossolalia because they are looking from the bottom up and because, in transposition, the higher is taking up the lower into itself, not acting in contradiction to it. Spiritual presence can never be discerned in any way but spiritually (18).

In his conclusion Lewis adds four additional points. First, his theory of transposition is not to be confused with the theory of "Developmentalism," which reverses the process. Millions of years of eating did not precede the Christian sacrament (18). Second, transposition helps explain the Incarnation. One of the creeds says that the Incarnation was accomplished "not by conversion of the Godhead into flesh, but by taking of the Manhood into God" (19).[1] Third, when looking from below, the materialist will have all the facts but none of the meaning. One will never see that there is something higher by focusing only on the lower (19). Finally, Lewis believes that what people experience in physical reality may be a real analogy of the spiritual; it may be symbolic or sacramental in the sense discussed above—symbolizing spiritual reality and, somehow, simultaneously being that reality.

In the idea of *Transposition*, then, Lewis is suggesting that many of our categories of thought—the very methods by which we view and think about the world—are probably skewed, especially when it comes to thinking about and seeing spiritual realities. And so in the sermon, Lewis would have us give serious consideration to three possibilities: that God is not as far off from us as we may think; that miracles may be far more common than we can see—in fact it may be possible to blind ourselves to seeing miracles when they happen; and that the distinctions we make between literal and symbolic things may not exist outside our own understanding—or they may be less distinct than we think they are.

1. The sixth-century Athanasian Creed. Lewis's friend Sister Penelope published her translation of Athanasius's *De Incarnatione* (1944) for which Lewis wrote an introduction (no longer in print—see works cited for a translation currently available).

CHAPTER 9

Sacrament and the Problem of Knowing

Some of what Sacramentalism is about was discussed in the last chapter as it is closely related to the concept of Transposition. That Lewis viewed reality sacramentally is significant not only for defining the real but also because it sheds light on Lewis's theory of knowing.

Celebrating the Physical

One important point in relation to his view of reality is that Lewis's sacramentalism represents a near opposite extreme to the Idealism he once held. Recall that at one time he believed that "Matter=Nature=Satan. And on the other side Beauty, the only spiritual & not-natural thing that I have yet found" (May 23, 1918, in *Collected Letters* 1: 371). This younger Lewis is very different from the Christian convert who described transcendent reality as the most concrete existence there is. Lewis's previous philosophical war with the flesh was not a part of his Christian way of thinking. Where other world views demand the total destruction of our nature (see Buddhism), Christianity only calls for a redirection, and "has no quarrel, like Plato, with the body as such, nor with the physical elements in our make-up" (*Pain* 104).

In *Letters to Malcolm,* Lewis values the physical body as unique among God's sentient creatures, saying that among beasts and angels, only people can praise God for the glory of Nature. Animals cannot appreciate it and angels are "pure intelligences. They *understand* colours and tastes better than our greatest scientists; but have they retinas or palates? I fancy the 'beauties of nature' are a secret God has shared with us alone" (17–18). Lewis believes the resurrection of the body is an important doctrine for this reason. Part of why we have been made is to praise those qualities of God's work that only our physical senses and reasoning minds combined can appreciate. Lewis valued the physical body and the whole of physical creation because he viewed reality sacramentally.

Symbol and Metaphor

We have seen Lewis describe this sacramental view in two passages. In *The Allegory of Love* he said that *allegory* is the act of using visible symbols to express our invisible concepts. *Symbolism* or *sacramentalism,* though, is the act of looking for a higher, invisible "something" in our own visible world. In "Transposition" Lewis says that earthly reality cannot only symbolize heavenly reality but also be something *of* that reality (15). For example, I suspect that the joy adults have in watching babies laugh or little children open Christmas presents is because their faces and enthusiasm mirror something of the heavenly reality Christ was referring to when he said in order to enter the kingdom of heaven, we must become like children (Matthew 18:3). This quality of finding reality within the symbol that at once also symbolizes the reality is what Lewis calls "sacramental" ("Transposition" 15).

Michael Edwards lays out a system for understanding the sacramental relationship between the heavenly and the earthly in his article, "C. S. Lewis: Imagining Heaven." In order to imagine heaven, he argues, we must first attend "to everyday earth" (114). Lewis does not doubt the reality of Earth, nor does he grudgingly bear it while waiting for heaven. He loves the real as he both knows and will come to know it. His vision of heaven is "both other and the same" (115). Heaven is our world, but our world as "enhanced . . . changed, as the more-than-real, as the really real." At the same time, Edwards realizes that Earth is not heaven. It provides "glimpses of heaven" (116). Therefore, we face the danger of loving the Earth too much so as to hold on to it "and resist God's calling of us towards the better earth of heaven" (121). But we shouldn't hate the Earth. Lewis says this is a distinctive view in Christianity: "Isn't Xtianity separated from the other religions just by the fact that it does not allow one to exclude or reject matter?" (February 5, 1945, in *Collected Letters* 2: 640). Edwards concludes that sacramentalism requires a balanced perspective. There is a sameness between heaven and Earth, and there is also an otherness.

Lewis makes a similar point when he talks about imagination and metaphor: In "On Stories," he describes how the imagination can grasp higher realities that reason can't. As examples, he points to stories like *Oedipus the King* and *The Hobbit*, stories of fulfilled prophecy that fill the reader with a feeling of awe because they set before our imaginations something that has always confused our intellects. In the story we are allowed to see how destiny and free will can combine, even how free will is the tool of destiny. The story does what philosophical explanation can't quite do. It may not be "like real life" on a surface level, but it shows us an image of what reality may well be like at some deeper level ("On Stories" 100–01).

The imagination is capable of doing, in part, what reason can't: enabling the knower to apprehend the deeper level or, as Lewis says it, "some more central region" (15). Notice the similarity between this image of levels of reality and Aslan's country in *The Last Battle*, which is at the center of many different realities.

Lewis carries this idea into our understanding of metaphors in *Miracles*:

> Grammatically the things we say of Him are "metaphorical": but in a deeper sense it is our physical and psychic energies that are mere "metaphors" of the real Life which is God. Divine Sonship is, so to speak, the solid of which biological sonship is merely a diagrammatic representation on the flat ... [It] is just the recognition of God's positive and concrete reality which the religious imagery preserves ... The ultimate spiritual reality is not vaguer, more inert, more transparent than the images, but more positive, more dynamic, more opaque ... Neither God nor even the gods are "shadowy" in traditional imagination: even the human dead, when glorified in Christ, cease to be "ghosts" and become "saints" ... If we must have a mental picture to symbolise Spirit, we should represent it as something *heavier* than matter. (122–23)

In other words, if we're going to talk about God, Jesus, or heaven, we're better off using words like *Father* than *Force*, *Son of Man* than *Imminent Presence*, or *City of Gold* than *Transcendent Realm*. Anytime we talk about God we'll use metaphors—better to use the kind that appeal to our sense

of solid reality than the ones that we mistakenly take as being more literal but that are in the end more like descriptions
of human ideas than Divine Realities.

In fact, in response to critics who wanted to *demythologize*
scripture, especially Rudolf Bultmann,[1] because its images
seemed primitive, unrealistic, and incapable of being literal,
Lewis said that human beings may "find the doctrines of the
Resurrection, the Ascension, and the Second Coming inadequate to our thoughts" ("Fern-seed and Elephants" 123). If we
do take them as inadequate, our likely response will be to say
they're unacceptable on a literal level but not on a symbolic
one. We can accept them as completely symbolic. But Lewis
would say this represents a mistake in our thinking. Lewis
summarizes the argument before pointing to the mistake:

> All the details are derived from our present experience; but
> the reality transcends our experience: therefore all the de-
> tails are wholly and equally symbolical. But suppose a dog
> were trying to form a conception of human life. All the de-
> tails in its picture would be derived from canine experience.
> Therefore all that the dog imagined could, at best, be only
> analogically true of human life. The conclusion is false. If
> the dog visualized our scientific researches in terms of rat-
> ting, this would be analogical; but if it thought that eating
> could be predicated of humans only in an analogical sense,
> the dog would be wrong. In fact if a dog could ... be plunged
> for a day into human life, it would be hardly more surprised
> by hitherto unimagined differences than by hitherto unsus-
> pected similarities ... But the dog can't get into human life.
> Consequently, though it can be sure that its best ideas of
> human life are full of analogy and symbol, it could never

1. Bultmann, *New Testament Mythology and Other Basic Writings*.

point to any one detail and say, "This is entirely symbolic."
("Fern-seed" 123–24)

It's the same way for us. Because we don't have access to
transcendent experience, we can't know which of our cur-
rent experiences are wholly symbolic, or which are partially
symbolic and partially literal.

If we sailed to the farthest reaches of space above our Earth
or dug down to its deepest center, we would never find our
way to heaven, and we would never dig ourselves down to
hell. But that doesn't mean heaven isn't somehow "up" and hell
somehow "down." We simply can't know which parts of our
symbols/metaphors about the Transcendent are wholly symbolic and which are or at least include the literal.

Lewis makes this very point in chapter 16 of *Miracles*. He
is discussing the nature of heaven, and specifically Christ's
ascension, when he says that, in viewing the ascension, the
disciples perceived Christ as both moving physically upward
into the blue sky and ascending into the spiritual realm,
the home of God (207). They did not distinguish between
the physical and spiritual acts of ascent. To do so gives rise,
Lewis argues, to a "literalism" that did not occur till the later
Middle Ages and the seventeenth century. In fact, the man
who genuinely thinks heaven to be in the sky may have in
his deepest self a more accurate and spiritual understanding
than the best of modern rationalists. The blending of the
ideas of God, heaven, and the blue sky is not accidental at all.
That we envision the sky as begetting and the Earth as bear-
ing is part and parcel with the imagination God gave us, with
the foreknowledge God had of "what the sky would mean
to us" (208). And if he knew, it wasn't an accident but an
intentional choice. Perhaps such meanings are part of what
the Earth was created for: to see with the imagination the

spiritual reality in the earthly image: "The ancients in letting the spiritual symbolism of the sky flow straight into their minds without stopping to discover by analysis that it was a symbol, were not entirely mistaken."

Lewis suggests the very way we think needs transformation—to become more sacramental:

> Our illness is that Spirit has been at war with Nature within us, and nothing in our current situation can heal us. But we do get glimpses that the healing will occur. The Sacraments, the sense-centered images used in poetry, the romance of the marriage bed, the beauty of the world—all these point to the sealing of the breach. But they are only hints. "Mystics have got as far in contemplation of God as the point at which the senses are banished" (209), but the point at which they will be brought back into place hasn't been reached by anyone.

In ignoring all images of heaven, a person makes a greater mistake than those who confuse the images for the reality. For they, at least, do not mistakenly associate spirit with abstraction. Lewis's solution involves the marriage of Spirit and Nature, not their divorce.

And this is not merely the case in terms of our own understanding, but it is the case in terms of what our heavenly future will actually be. Lewis says that most of what we know about the New Creation is explained in metaphor, but not all of it. The Resurrection makes that clear. The resurrected Christ appeared in specific places, ate, and allowed Himself to be touched. So whatever our New Nature in Christ will be, it touches, it interlocks with, the Old Nature. Because the New is new and beyond our experience, we have to think about it metaphorically, but because it also interlocks with the Old, "some facts about it come through into our present experience in all their literal facthood" (*Miracles* 202).

Lewis's sacramental view of heaven and Earth, then, leads us to thinking about a sacramental view of God. Leann Payne crystalizes the argument by beginning with Lewis's claim in *Miracles* that God is the most concrete thing there is and the most basic fact. From there she argues that "while it is impossible that our anthropomorphic images of God can fully reflect His presence within, without, and all about us, our abstractions of Him can be even more harmfully misleading" (Payne, *Real Presence* 17). She defends this view by referring to *Letters to Malcolm*: "What soul ever perished for believing that God the Father really has a beard?" (22). Anthropomorphizing God is not an answer to knowing him, but abstraction is worse! Says Payne, "our fear of naive anthropomorphism should never drive us to a degree of theological abstraction that becomes a substitute for receiving experientially Reality Himself" (18).

Lewis says this in his essay, "Is Theology Poetry?," where he makes an argument similar to the one in the "Fern-seed" essay quoted above. There Lewis was saying that the distinction we make between literal and figurative language is modern, not biblical. Here he argues that *any* language we use to talk about God, or any other aspect of transcendent reality will *always* be figurative, that is, metaphorical: "We can, if you like, say 'God entered history' instead of saying 'God came down to earth'. But, of course, 'entered' is just as metaphorical as 'came down'. You have only substituted horizontal or undefined movement for vertical movement. We can make our language duller; we cannot make it less metaphorical" ("Is Theology Poetry?" 80).

Planetary Sacrament

A sacramental view explains how, in *Perelandra*, Ransom comes to the realization that the battle against the Un-man must be carried into physical confrontation, the *real* world, which Ransom amazingly sees as also a world of *myth*. The theme is a repeated one, as noted by James Como: "In *Perelandra*, when the protagonist Ransom begins to lose the debate with the Un-man; in *The Silver Chair*, when the Witch's word-enchantment has nearly brought success; when all the Voluble Selves of *The Great Divorce* are about to rhetorize their way back to hell—in each of these cases, Lewis abandons argument for action, remonstration for demonstration" ("Introduction" xxviii). Ransom has come to planet Venus to war against a demonic emissary called the "Un-man." The latter is there to tempt the newly born Eve of that planet to sin, while Ransom is there to prevent it. As the war of wit with the Un-man proceeds, Ransom realizes that he cannot compete against a creature who needs no sleep and who has lies and half-truths as part of his arsenal. Ransom knows that, if the temptation is allowed to continue, the Eve of Perelandra will eventually succumb.

Twice the thought comes to Ransom that "this can't go on" (109, 114). After the idea comes to him a third time (119), Ransom finally realizes that the thought is not his own but is a command of God. He wonders what he can do and begins to rationalize that God will take care of things and that he (Ransom) was probably just sent there to observe the triumph over evil which he would return to Earth to report.

Having thought that his—that humankind's—struggle with demonic powers was a *"spiritual* struggle" not a physical one, Ransom is at first relieved, but he is also imaginatively honest enough to realize that he fears fighting the Un-man

(*Perelandra* 122). Ransom is certain (for a moment) that God does not intend that he face such a conflict, that to consider a physical struggle against Satan would be to "degrade the spiritual warfare to the condition of mere mythology." It is at this moment that Ransom has a revelation: in an unfallen world, myth, truth, and fact lose distinction. The sacraments on Earth are a sign that such distinctions there are part of the fall and will be done away, and he realizes that "whatever happened here [on Perelandra] would be of such a nature that earth-men would call it mythological." Having believed all his life in the spiritual significance of the Incarnation, he is now awakened to its physical or sacramental significance where, on a perfect planet, all those who stand for Maleldil [God] are types of the Incarnation. Ransom learns to reimagine his faith, his place; it comes to him in an overwhelming final revelation: "It is not for nothing that you are named Ransom" (125). He realizes that he is there to be the hand of the great Divine Ransom. Thus realizing, he obeys and confronts the *Un-man* in physical combat. Fact in this context clearly indicates a connection between knowing and doing. Ransom comes to understand that for truth to win out over the lies of the Un-man, it must be acted out and physically defended. In other words, knowing reality requires right action *in* and *toward* reality.

Sacrament and Heaven

As we've seen throughout this book, Lewis believes that the highest reality is the most concrete of all. He writes that our present bodies are "half phantasmal" in comparison to the spiritual bodies to come (August 19, 1947, in *Collected Letters*2: 1574). He makes it an important image in *Out of the Silent*

Planet when he describes the eldila (angels) who bathe in light and see physical creatures (like us) as ghostlike (94–95). And, of course, Lewis makes concrete higher reality the controlling image of *The Great Divorce*. Additionally, it appears several times in *Mere Christianity* and especially in *Miracles*: "If anything is to exist at all, then the Original Thing must be, not a principle nor a generality, much less an 'ideal' or a 'value,' but an utterly concrete fact" (116), and "God is basic Fact or Actuality, the source of all other facthood. At all costs therefore He must not be thought of as a featureless generality. If He exists at all, He is the most concrete thing there is" (121).

In *Miracles* Lewis contrasts the physical quality of both the Incarnation and the Resurrection with the contemporary conception of heaven as "a risen life which is purely 'spiritual' in the negative sense of that word: that is, we use the word 'spiritual' to mean not what it is but what it is not. We mean a life without space, without history, without environment, with no sensuous elements in it" (193). Lewis rejects this vision of heaven. These references speak specifically to the problem of equating spirit with merely abstract ideas. But this approach is, for Lewis, a complete reversal of the real.

In *Letters to Malcolm*, Lewis imagines what it would possibly be like to see heaven, saying it's like watching nature rise from the grave. What was momentary is now permanent. What was becoming is now simply being. What was subjective is now objective. The "hills and valleys of Heaven will be to those you now experience not as a copy is to an original, nor as a substitute is to the genuine article, but as the flower to the root, or the diamond to the coal" (123). The vision is sacramental. And so, the deeper we get into Lewis's view of reality, the "further in," to echo *The Last Battle*, the "further up" we need to look. Sacrament calls us to the reality of heaven.

CHAPTER 10

Lewis's Vision of Heaven

In a book about C. S. Lewis's theory of reality, a capstone chapter on the nature of heaven, is a must since, as his Mac-Donald character noted in *The Great Divorce*, "Heaven is reality itself" (70). An eighteen-year-old arrives at college to study education. She believes she'll someday be a teacher. But what drives her to work hard day after day for four years are those moments in which she imagines her future, sees herself in front of a classroom talking passionately about history or the mysteries of science, sees herself saving an at-risk kid who doesn't drop out but goes on to graduate and thanks that teacher who made a difference in his life with a big bear hug after the ceremony. Imagining the future motivates the education student to pursue her future. C. S. Lewis understood that imagining what heaven might be like was important to motivating Christians to endure a lifetime of waiting for that best of all promised goals, and so he envisioned heaven in numerous writings and in several ways. Some of what follows we've already covered, but I want to condense it so that we see its unified quality: a vision of the most real thing there is.

The More Real the Merrier

In *The Great Divorce*, Lewis paints a picture in which the closer we get to God, the more *real* everything gets. Hell (the farthest place from God) is smaller than a pebble on Earth and smaller than an atom in heaven (*Divorce* 138). When souls first arrive in heaven, their appearance is as ghosts. Their forms have been expanded, like blowing up a balloon, so that they match the size of things in heaven, but they are like empty air. A body is outlined, but they are transparent and so weightless that they cannot bend the grass beneath their feet, nor sink in water, nor pick up a heavenly apple from the ground. They look like "stains on the brightness of that air" (20). Those residents of heaven who come to greet the ghosts have been filled with the fullness of God's Divine Being. They are not ghosts in this tale but fully realized spirits. As God is more solid than anything on Earth in Lewis's vision, so these people are more solid, more real, and now more fully human than any human being in our world. The ghosts at the edge of heaven are given the chance to go further in and be filled like their heavenly counterparts.

Here then is a core Lewis image: heaven and heavenly beings are more solid than are we and the Earth we live on. We are ghosts and shadows and our world but a cheap copy of the heavenly one to come, like a landscape painting compared to the real place. In *Out of the Silent Planet*, the Sorn Augray describes the angelic perspective, noting that human beings are barely visible to them, and light, which seems hardly present to humans as a physical thing, is something the angels swim through (95). In *The Last Battle*, the friends of Narnia enter into heaven only to find that it's a new Narnia, like the old one, only bigger, but not really bigger—better to say *fuller*, more complete. As one of them puts it, it's "More like the real thing" (210). And because it's more real than our world, everything in it means so much more than things do here. If you've ever had an experience so wonderful that it made you think, "This is how things ought to be in real life," maybe you've experienced a taste of heaven, a place compared to which, Lewis says, our own world is just "shadowlands." So, Lewis first imagines for us a heaven that is more real than anything we've ever experienced on Earth.

The Feeling Intellect

In "Myth Became Fact," we encountered a dilemma about how we know things. On the one hand we can think about things, and on the other we can experience them, but we cannot do both at the same time (e.g., we can laugh at a joke or think about why it's funny but can't do both simultaneously). Thinking is careful and clear but lacks the concrete intensity of experience. Experience is intensely real but lacks the care and clarity of thinking. We all know the phrase, "we learn from experience," but that's not completely true. Lewis notes in *Pilgrim's Regress* that some people remain inattentive to the lessons of experience all their lives and so never learn from them (203). We've got to think about the things we do, but on the other hand we can't just sit around thinking all the time. God wants us to know him, not just know about him. And he wants us to act as he called Ransom to action in *Perelandra*.

Several times, then, Lewis suggests that heaven will be a place where thinking and experiencing come together. On Earth we think about what love is; in heaven Love is a Person we can experience. On Earth we read books *about* many different things, especially God, on the one hand, while some of our experiences of him are so intense that we cannot put them into words; in heaven the Divine Word speaks to us face to face in a language that lets us both hear and say every-thing we never could before. In heaven, to think a thing will be to do it; to do a thing will involve knowing it completely. On Earth our words are abstract expressions that never quite say everything we want them to. In heaven language is a Person, and to communicate will be to offer everything we are and to receive back every thought, feeling, and meaning from those with whom we share words.

In order to grasp an image of this idea, think about the dif-ferent ways we say, "I love you," to someone. When we're talk-ing on the phone with family and just hanging up or when we're leaving the house to go to work, we say, "I love you," or "Love you, bye." It's sincere, but it's not intense. It's not a lie, but it's just a routine. Then there are the times someone, say in the family, does something nice for us: the kids cook breakfast on a morning after a nightmarish day, the gift your spouse has been wanting for months finally arrives for his or her birth-day, a big surprise makes someone shout with excitement. In these moments, we say "I love you" as an expression of deep appreciation, surprised joy. Then there are the times we say, "I love you" to someone who has impacted us so profoundly that we have to hold back tears to say it. It's often at a major transition moment: a graduating student to a teacher; a son at the end of a visit to his ninety-year-old dad, knowing this may be the last time he sees him in this life; a mother to her son as she turns to leave from helping him set up his dorm room for his first year in college; a daughter to her father just before the wedding march begins. Think about all of these ex-amples. Now collect them together in your mind. Toss them in a bowl and mix them well—all these meanings in a simple three-word phrase. Drink from the bowl, and then speak the words, "I love you," with all those meanings coming out all at once. That's what a casual conversation in heaven will be like. Every time we speak.

Glory in Dreams Come True

At the end of the movie *Field of Dreams*, Ray Kinsella asks his father, "Is there a heaven?" The dad replies, "Oh yes. It's the place where dreams come true." C. S. Lewis would not say that we get everything we ever wanted in heaven (like the chance to play baseball again), but he does say that heaven is a place where the desire, the longing that accompanies our earthly dreams, is fulfilled when the glory of God enters into and transforms us.

In an earlier chapter we reviewed Lewis's most famous sermon, "The Weight of Glory." It gives us something of Lewis's vision of heaven. Recall that, for Lewis, glory means two things. First, it means "good report with God, acceptance by God, response, acknowledgement, and welcome into the heart of things" (15). Paul says that those who love God "will be known by Him (I Cor. 8:3)" ("The Weight of Glory" 15), but those who reject God will be rejected by him: "I never knew you. Depart from me." They will be "both banished from the presence of Him who is present everywhere and erased from the knowledge of Him who knows all . . . finally and unspeakably ignored."

How many trophies from your childhood do you have sitting in a closet or an attic right now? When you won those trophies, they were the most meaningful things in the world in those moments. Now they gather dust or don't see the light of day. We spend all our lives looking for approval. It's not just a "kids'" thing. Adults spend decades trying to win approval in their careers, their neighborhoods, their churches, their lodges, their country clubs, their online posts, their adult league sports. The boss says, "Good job," the guys admire the new car, the church folks love the dessert you brought to potluck. But the satisfaction that comes from these moments of approval fades, and we toss the ribbons or trophies into the closet, buy the next new thing to keep up with the Joneses, or take a thousand pictures on our next vacation to post them on social media so our "friends" can tell us how lucky and awesome we are. The approval fades, and we keep running the hamster wheel, failing to realize the truth: we're chasing temporary approval because we're meant for the true eternal version of it. Once we realize that—that what we most want is to hear God say, "Well done"—we start to seek that approval, the one that really matters, the one that will never go away. All other approvals fade from our joy because they're as temporary as anything else on the Earth. But when God says, "Well done, my good and faithful servant," it's an eternal, infinite, omnipotent approval. It lasts forever, and its joy never fades from our recognition. Heaven is the place where we can stop trying to find someone or something that will tell us we're good enough. God has been telling us all along, but we'll finally believe him to the very core of our souls.

The second thing glory means for Lewis is entering into God's beauty. Here is where we see the idea of dreams coming true; it's connected to Lewis's idea of *longing*. The lesson here is for our imaginations, so I want to conjure some experiential images: Have you ever had moments in life that felt magical? Have you ever been so head over heels in love you could hardly eat? Ever wondered just how big your grin can get when you watch your kids open their birthday presents? Have you ever seen a sunset so beautiful you thought you were seeing the light of God? I once saw the Grand Canyon but for only fifteen minutes. It had me in the first five seconds. I've seen dolphins swimming against a sunset in an ocean bay and snow falling through sunbeams, making rainbow colors as it floated to the ground. I've seen autumn trees so beautiful they broke my heart with Joy. We live in a world of magic.

But we also live in another world. Your parents and teachers called it "The Real World," constantly threatened you with it, and constantly dashed your dreams with it. Earlier we saw how this language is a lie foisted on us by Screwtape. But even so, the world often disappoints us, and we long for a better one. We live in a world where we have to work, study for tests, clean the house; where lovers and family break our hearts; where boredom sets in, and fun never lasts; and where a lot of the things we want to do in life never happen. We want to live in the magical world, but we never get to stay there and, worse, we end up spending most of our time in this ho-hum world, which seems to us anything *but* real.

Two worlds: One we spend most of our time in, and one we wish we could. We wish for life to be "magical" all the time. We wish for the honeymoon to last forever, for the post–Thanksgiving dinner siesta in the recliner to be a daily occurrence, for every movie we see (and every moment in life) to be just as good as *Star Wars* was. We long for 2 A.M. conversations in dark dorm rooms lit by lava lamps—RUSH's 2112 album playing in the background—conversations at one moment profound, and the next profusely stupid.

"The Weight of Glory" tells us that people have a desire for the magical moments in life. But those moments never last. The magical moments in life are the glorious moments in life. They are the moments we feel like life was really made for, but they are moments that never last long because those glorious moments are gifts to us from God, tastes of the glory he's promised to give us in heaven.

When we experience it briefly on Earth in some form that's just a shadow of God's real glory (a shadow of that joy is probably all we could take of it), we get a hunger for it. And in Christ we get a hope—the hope that one day we will see that glory face to face. All the glorious things we've ever hoped for on Earth are pale shadows by comparison. In life, almost all of our dreams will never come true (though some of them might). When we see God's face and he fills us with his glory, his magical essence, the fullness of his being (his reality), the feeling we'll feel will be *like* all our dreams coming true but with an intensity times a thousand. All our old earthly joys and dreams will feel like cheap substitutes, and in that Presence of glory a thought will come as we cry happy tears: *"This was it all along. This is what I've been searching for all my life!"*

And this time we'll get to keep it. This time it will never go away.

The Literal Metaphor: The Body of Christ

Lewis's idea of Transposition also informs his view of heaven. If you know music, you understand the idea of transposing a song from a major key to a minor one. Lewis uses this idea to explain life in heaven. He sees some qualities in human life as "minor key" versions of the major heavenly key. Lewis pictures this idea of "transposition" in *Mere Christianity* using geometry.

Notice that a line shows us one direction of space (up and down), that a square shows us two directions of space (up and down and side to side, and that a cube shows us three directions (up and down, side to side, and near to far). Also notice that a square is made of four lines and a cube is made

up of six squares. The higher, more complex object takes up the Lower simpler ones into itself.[1]

I apply Lewis this way: Say that the line equals the building blocks of the universe, energy and matter. Say then that the square equals living things like plants and animals, which are made up of matter. Say, finally, that the cube equals human beings; we are made of matter, we are alive, and we have something more that animals don't have: personality. We think, speak, love, admire beauty, make things, and choose to do right or wrong.

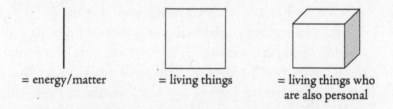

= energy/matter   = living things   = living things who
                                                    are also personal

Now we don't know what the life of God is like in heaven, but, just as people take energy and life into themselves, so God must also take these *and* personality up into himself as part of his heavenly life. So, some of what we experience on Earth is going to be similar to what we will experience in heaven, and maybe there are some clues to these similarities.

But then there should also be some radical differences too. I can't imagine what would be next up from a cube (I've

1. Lewis's use of geometric shapes to illustrate levels of reality comes from Edwin A. Abbott's *Flatland*.

heard it's called a tesseract). We don't have four dimensions of space (only height, width, and depth) and so can't readily think beyond solid objects like cubes or spheres. An object at the next level up would have to be called an "extra solid" or something. I also can't imagine what the next step up from human personality is either, but the Bible hints at it in passages like John 1:1: "In the beginning was the word and the word was with God and the word was God." From this and other passages in scripture, Christians have discerned the idea of the Trinity, which Lewis calls the "Super Personal." Animals are alive. People are alive and have personality. The next step up, according to Lewis, is a living, personal God, who is Super Personal: He is three persons, but only one person. One God, but Father, Son, and Holy Spirit. And of course, we can't imagine it; it totally confuses us. But, again, maybe we get hints of what it's like here on Earth.

Human beings are individual, but we live in groups. We have individual personalities, but we act and think as Americans or Irish, Southerners or Yankees, Christians or Buddhists. Sometimes, though, our groups become so tight-knit that they take on a personality. Think of being in a music group or choir or on a sports team. When I was a soccer coach, I noticed that, by the end of a soccer season, my players were so tight-knit that they started to talk alike, think alike, predict one another's movements as if they could read one another's minds. There's a bond, a unity that sports people call "team spirit." But it's not like they really become one personality, and there's no real spirit hovering over the team. It might seem more literal to us when we think about a couple who has been married for a long time. We can often tell when two people have been married for thirty or forty years: they finish each other's sentences, they communicate with facial expressions, they even almost look alike. The Bible says the two "become one flesh" (Genesis 2:24). But obviously they're not one person, right? We can tell that easily enough when they have a fight. This symbol of union on Earth, though, may become a reality in heaven (and even on Earth it is sacramentally more than just a symbol). We have seen Lewis's idea that what is metaphorical here on Earth may be more literal in heaven. So perhaps in heaven God, who is spirit, experiences in his three-in-one personality a genuine spiritual connection, a team spirit, or better a unifying Spirit that is so real, so literal, that it *is* one of the three, and it makes the *three* into a real *one*, and they are both at the same time. In people you get strong individuality. But in God you get total individuality and total unity simultaneously. But how does this add to our understanding of heaven?

For Lewis, the biblical metaphor that says Christians are the "body of Christ," stops being symbolic and becomes in some way literal in the higher heavenly reality. In heaven, Christians will be unified with Christ after the same pattern that is in the Trinity. To explain this, Lewis, in *Mere Christianity*, talks about the difference between "begetting" and "making" (see book 4, chapter 1). A sculptor can *make* a statue, but he *begets* children. To beget is to make something *like yourself*. Now one of the promises to Christians in the New Testament is that they will become sons of God (Galatians 3:26). But isn't everyone already? Isn't God the father of Christians and non-Christians alike? He argues that Jesus is the "only begotten Son" of God (John 3:16). He is the only one who is *like* God. We are *made* by God but only become *begotten* of God when we enter into the Super Personal life of Christ, when we become part of his living body. Apart from Christ we are like dead statues, though lovingly made by the sculptor's hand. The promise of sonship is the promise that the statues will come to life. People become begotten of God by becoming like him, by entering into his life, his body, what Lewis called the "Zoe" life of Christ in which people themselves become little Christs.

Lewis is not saying that people become God in heaven. What humanity enters in heaven is a participatory life modeled after the Trinity: we never stop being ourselves, creatures of God who owe him worship; in fact, Lewis suggests that the goal of spiritual perfection is for us to become more ourselves than we ever were before (*Mere Christianity* 190), yet we become unified to each other and to Christ in a way that makes something like "team spirit" a reality. We are in Christ, and he is in us, and we are in each other in heaven (see John 14–17). We fill him up and he is our fullness forever (Ephesians 1:23).

Imagine what it must be like to see your friends, your relatives, your spouse in heaven—to recognize them for who they are as individuals but to know them so personally, so intimately, that to talk to them is to share thoughts rather than words. Think about that space you have felt between you and your father because his generation is different from yours. Think about the space, the distance, you have felt from your best friend in the world when you wanted to tell him or her about the secret sorrow you've been hiding in your heart, but you just didn't know how to begin. Think about how happy your husband or wife has made you, how you have longed to speak it, to share every thought, picture, and feeling whirling around in your head, too fast and too intense to put it all into words, how words are not even enough to say everything you could to your partner of five or fifty years.

Then imagine a heaven in which those distances disappear completely, where to speak a word is to know someone's heart, where I know all whom I have ever loved (and more) as I know myself (and better than I know myself here on Earth) because I am no longer just me: I am me, in them, in

Christ, who is in me. All united together, never lonely again. That's what unity in Christ means. That's what C. S. Lewis says heaven is like.

Answers to Everything

Job faced terrible suffering and wanted to know why. He complained to God constantly (Job 7:17–20) and demanded an audience to plead his case (23:3–7). Eventually God appeared to stifle Job's presumption, saying, "Who is this that darkens counsel by words without knowledge?" (38:2). God spends the next four chapters talking to Job. But God doesn't explain why Job has suffered. He bombards Job with questions that point out just how big God is and how small Job. In the end Job realizes that he has no position from which to argue with God. But he doesn't give in because he has been bullied. He repents and accepts because he has seen God and, by seeing, knows who and what it is that he's dealing with:

> "[You asked,] 'Who is this that obscures my counsel with-
>   out knowledge?'
> Surely I spoke of things I did not understand,
> things too wonderful for me to know.
> My ears had heard of you
> but now my eyes have seen you.
> Therefore I despise myself
> and repent in dust and ashes." (Job 42:3, 5–6)

Lewis comes to the same conclusion at the end of *Till We Have Faces*. Though the gods of the book are pagan, the message of the story for moderns is quite clear. The queen of Glome, Orual, is angry at Divinity for a life of bitter loneliness and lost love. She writes a book, her case against the gods, in which she demands an explanation for her suffering—for the unjust manner in which she has been treated. In the end, as with Job, she is not given answers, only an experience of the power, the beauty, the glory of the Divine presence. And that is enough. She sees her own sin—the lies she has hidden from herself—and she sees the god of the mountain for who he is and concludes, "I ended my [complaint against you] with the words *no answer*. I know now, Lord, why you utter no answer. You are yourself the answer. Before your face questions die away" (308).

People of all faiths and no faith alike have often longed to ask God questions, especially questions about why things happened in their lives the way they did—why a loved one died or an accident happened, or why a job fell through or a marriage didn't last. Lewis understood that one of the great promises of heaven is that all our questions will be answered when we get there, not because God will tell us what happened, or why, but because he *is* the answer. Revelation 22:4 promises that we "shall see His face." And that will be answer enough.

Heavenly Praise

Lewis described heaven in a variety of his writings, from direct examples like *The Great Divorce*, to comparative examples like the Utter East of the Narnian world in *The Voyage of the Dawn Treader*. Here I am pleased to offer, for the first time in print, one more heavenly description from Lewis's hand.

The passage has to do with the need to praise. Lewis takes up the issue of praise in *Reflections on the Psalms*. In that book, he raises the question, why would God want us to praise him? After all, "We all despise the man who demands continued assurance of his own virtue, intelligence or delightfulness; we despise still more the crowd of people round every dictator, every millionaire, every celebrity, who gratify that demand" (Psalms 77). The solution is that praise isn't something God needs from us. It's something we need to give (80–81). People experience this in life all the time: if you've ever been to a really good restaurant or seen a movie you absolutely loved, you've told people about it. You praised the food or the film. In fact, Lewis says praise is necessary because it "completes the enjoyment" of the thing we've experienced (81). Until you've told people about it, you're not really done enjoying it.

And so it will be with God in heaven. Lewis's first attempt at a book on prayer resulted in a handful of looseleaf, handwritten sheets. In one part of this unpublished document, Lewis wrote about the impulse to praise, and he tried to describe it in terms of the need to praise God—the fulfillment that praising him will bring in heaven. In so doing, he rendered a vision of Longing and how that desire—fulfilled when we see God—leads to soul-fulfilling praise. The vision is beautiful. Here it is, as I said, for the first time in print:

> Sometimes one can explain a real thing only by first describing something imaginary, and that is what I am now going to do. I hope you will have patience if I seem to be taking a long time. For the matter is important. To understand about the Praise or Adoration of God is more important than any of the things you were going to ask God to give you, more important, in a sense, than your own Salvation. At least "Salvation," if you could have it without this, would be no good to you ...
>
> Picture a vast open space where creatures of all sorts, including Man but some of them far higher, stronger, more ancient and godlike than he, stand in a circle; waiting. Though the assembly is so great (millions upon millions) there is

perfect silence, for they are all expecting something. At last, suddenly, it is there in the midst. I cannot, even by imagination, suggest what it appears like to the nonhuman spectators; except that it is their heart's desire. And I can suggest only very dimly how it appears to the men and women and children. It is in one way like a physical sensation: like fresh air with garden smells in it after you have been long shut up in a stuffy room; like the ease that comes when you take off an uncomfortable pair of shoes; like cool water rippling round hot feet or warm water embracing cold ones; like the blessed emptiness in the place where a sharp pain was, now that the pain has gone. In a word it is like relief, like everything which would make you say "It's alright *now.*" In another way, however, it is more like a kind of knowledge than a kind of sensation: like the moment when you first see, in one glorious flash, the answer to a problem you have been working on for years, and see, almost in the same flash, how this is going to be the answer to a whole series of other problems (which you thought quite unconnected) and how perfectly it fits in with everything else you know. And you wonder how you could have been so dense as not to see it before. Now at last you can really get on . . . Once again you will say "It's alright *now.* I see *Now.*" All your thinking, up till that moment, will appear to have been fumbling and groping and misapprehension. Now the real clue has been put into your hand. You can go on and on now; no more dead-ends, no more false trails: you have a master-secret and it is going to lead to—well, literally, to everything. But then, in yet another way, this thing that has appeared is more like beauty than it is like knowledge. All that ever led you on mile after mile among the mountains, all that rushes back on your mind at the smell of the sea, all that you ever felt during those few perfect moments (and they are very few) when great music or great verse was having its completest effect upon you, so that you ceased to be aware of yourself at all, all that, and more, comes full upon those who see this thing. All, and more: it is obvious now that all the other beauties were only shreds and echoes and copies of this. This is where they all came from; this is the real thing at last. If you were allowed to enjoy it for a thousand years you would not notice the passage of time. And yet again, this thing is like love. It is like coming home to the faces and voices and the very smells and sounds you love best, after long, lonely years in some cruel country, perhaps in a prison camp. It is like meeting again your best beloved, whom you thought to be dead, or with whom you had quarreled, and finding that all is well. You see now why I cannot describe it. For though, in one sense, it is most certainly like all the things I have suggested, yet after all it is utterly unlike them. All these remind you of it; yet when it appears it is overwhelmingly new. It gives you experiences so new that it has to give you new modes of sensation to receive them. It opens a new world, outside and beyond all that you have known. It satisfies desires which you never knew you had. If I could really describe it, my words would break like the heart of everyone who read them. But of course it is impossible for any man to describe it . . . But try to accept (only as an imagination) the idea that its coming fills all that assembly of creatures with utter satisfaction of all their known, and unknown, desires; that when they see it they become themselves for the first time, and know beyond doubt that this is the thing they were made for.

You will not find it hard to suppose that when it appeared some sound would break from the lips of all those creatures: perhaps just a long inarticulate *Oh*.

Now that sound, the delight of the creatures made audible, may stand as our first crude idea of Praise. For the Christian doctrine is that at the back of everything, in the heart of everything, there is a Being of absolute beauty, the heart's desire of all the creatures He has made. And we have been made in order that we might thus meet Him. And the inevitable result of that meeting, on our part, is that we should praise or adore. ("Prayer Manuscript" 10–11)

Lewis will go on to say that, if we couldn't praise God when we encounter him in heaven, it would actually bother us, it would "be a kind of stifling and torture" (11).

What else is there to say about reality having concluded with the reality of heaven? Perhaps only this reminder: If God is the most real thing there is, and if God is Infinite, without limits, then heaven for us will be an eternal encounter with that which will become more and more real to us throughout our eternal lives. The pursuit of God is nothing less than this: the greatest, most complete pursuit of Reality, the only one that can somehow become yet "Greatest-er," the only one that, upon completion, will never end.

Further up, and further in.

Appendix

Terms for Reality in Lewis's Writings

As noted in chapter 2, the primary synonym for the word *reality* in Lewis's works is the word *fact*, a word that Lewis uses in a straightforward, consistent manner; however, other synonyms that Lewis uses, including *event, existence, history,* and, to a lesser extent, *nature,* don't carry quite the comprehensive scope of the words *reality* and *fact*.

1. *FACT:* The essay "Myth Became Fact" and the book *Miracles* are the richest resources for the term *fact* and its synonyms in Lewis's writings. In "Myth Became Fact," we saw that truth is about reality, and reality the thing that truth is about (66). Consider a similar passage from *Miracles:* "Events in general are not 'about' anything and cannot be true or false" (27). Taken together, these two texts make it apparent that the word *reality* is synonymous with *fact* in Lewis's thinking. If there is a distinction to be made, however, it is probably that sometimes Lewis takes *fact* as referencing the whole of *reality,* but sometimes he focuses on individual elements or *facts* within *reality,* especially the *facts* of science or *events* of *history,* thus using the word less comprehensively (see below).

2. *EXISTENCE:* In *Miracles,* Lewis writes that "concrete, individual, determinate things do now exist"; these "are not mere principles or generalities or theorems, but things—facts—real, resistant existences" (115). Shortly thereafter, he refers to the "brute fact of existence, the fact that it is actually there and is itself." Overall, the word *existence* seems synonymous with *reality* in Lewis's writing.

3. *HISTORY:* In chapter 15 of *Miracles* Lewis connects the words *fact* and *history* (176n). And in a letter to Arthur Greeves, he writes, "The pagan stories are God expressing Himself through the minds of poets, using such images as He found there, while Christianity is God expressing Himself through what we call 'real things'" (October 18, 1931, in *Collected Letters* 1: 977). But Lewis tends to relegate the word *history* to the facts of Earth— to events that have taken place on Earth, not in heaven (see *Nature* below). And so, the word is not as comprehensive in referring to *reality.*

4. *MYTH:* Lewis makes an unusual distinction between heavenly and earthly reality in "Myth Became Fact" with interesting connections to the words *history* and *nature.* In the essay he writes, "the heart of Christianity is a myth which is also a fact. The old myth of the dying god ... comes down from the heaven of legend and imagination to the earth of history. It happens—at a particular date, in a particular place, followed by definable historical consequences" (66).

What's interesting here is that *myth* gets associated with heaven and *fact/history* with Earth or the world of *nature.* Thus, Lewis thought heaven was the most real place there is, and he also considered heaven to be mythic. What's immediately important here is the way

Lewis distinguishes between heavenly and earthly reality, between the supernatural and the natural.

5. *NATURE:* Lewis will tend to use words like *history* (as noted above) and *event* to refer to actions that have taken place in created *nature* (our universe). The word *existence* appears as a synonym for *reality,* and *facts* are elements of or actions in reality but with a focus, again, on *nature.* In *Miracles* Lewis says that what the "Naturalist believes is that the ultimate Fact, the thing you can't go behind, is a vast process in space and time which is *going on of its own accord*" (14). In other words, the ultimate fact is nature. But Lewis does not accept this, arguing that "Nature is a *creature,* a created thing, with its own particular tang or flavour" (87). As such, it is created fact. He claims that "God is basic Fact" (121), that the "Supernaturalist agrees with the Naturalist that there must be something which exists in its own right; some basic Fact" (15). The Supernaturalist, moreover, believes that facts fall into two categories. In the first category is the "One Thing which is basic and original, which exists on its own." In the second category are things that exist because of the One Thing (God): "The one basic Thing has caused all other things to be. It exists on its own; they exist because it exists" (15). Lewis says that the Naturalist thinks nature is "the ultimate and self existent Fact" (87), whereas the Supernaturalist thinks "God is basic Fact or Actuality" and "the source of all other facthood" (121). Elsewhere in *Miracles* Lewis calls God the "fountain of facthood" (117). Thus, it is clear that although *nature* is not a perfect synonym for *reality,* nevertheless there is a connection because all facts, including nature, derive from the one fact (God).

6. *SUMMARY:* In Lewis's writings,

a. Reality, Fact, and Existence appear to be synonymous.
b. Myth seems primarily regulated to transcendent reality.
c. History, Event, and Nature focus on created reality—reality here on Earth.

Works Cited

Works by Lewis

Lewis, C. S. *The Abolition of Man.* Collier, 1955.

——. *The Allegory of Love: A Study in Medieval Tradition.* 1936. Oxford UP, 1958.

——. *The Collected Letters of C. S. Lewis.* Vol. 1, *Family Letters, 1905–1931.* Edited by Walter Hooper, Harper Collins, 2000.

——. *The Collected Letters of C. S. Lewis.* Vol. 2, *Books, Broadcasts, and the War, 1931–1949.* Edited by Walter Hooper, Harper Collins, 2004.

——. *The Collected Letters of C. S. Lewis.* Vol. 3, *Narnia, Cambridge and Joy, 1950–1963.* Edited by Walter Hooper, Harper Collins, 2006.

——. *The Dark Tower. The Dark Tower and Other Stories.* Edited by Walter Hooper, Harcourt Brace, 1977, pp. 15–98.

——. "De Futilitate." *Essay Collection & Other Short Pieces,* edited by Lesley Walmsley, Harper Collins, 2000, pp. 669–81.

——. *The Discarded Image: An Introduction to Medieval and Renaissance Literature.* Cambridge UP, 1964.

"Dogma and the Universe." *Essay Collection & Other Short Pieces,* edited by Lesley Walmsley, Harper Collins, 2000, pp. 118–26.

——. "Dungeon Grates." *The Collected Poems of C. S. Lewis,* edited by Walter Hooper, Fount, 1994, pp. 184–85.

———. "Edmund Spenser 1552–99." *Studies in Medieval and Renaissance Literature*, edited by Walter Hooper, Cambridge UP, 1966, pp. 121–45.

———. *Essay Collection and Other Short Pieces*. Edited by Lesley Walmsley, Harper Collins, 2000.

———. *An Experiment in Criticism*. Cambridge UP, 1961.

"Fern-seed and Elephants." *Fern-seed and Elephants and Other Essays on Christianity*. Fontana, 1975, pp. 104–25.

———. *The Great Divorce*. HarperCollins, 1973.

———. *A Grief Observed*. HarperCollins, 1989.

———. *The Horse and His Boy*. HarperCollins, 1954.

———. "Is Theology Poetry?" *Socratic Digest*, edited by Joel D. Heck, Concordia UP, 2012, pp. 75–82.

———. *The Last Battle*. HarperCollins, 1956.

———. *Letters of C. S. Lewis*. Rev. and enlarged ed. Edited by W. H. Lewis. Rev. ed. edited by Walter Hooper, Harvest/HBJ, 1993.

———. *Letters to an American Lady*. Edited by Clyde S. Kilby, Eerdmans, 1994.

———. *Letters to Malcolm: Chiefly on Prayer*. Harvest/HBJ, 1964.

———. "Light." *Light: C. S. Lewis's First and Final Short Story*, by Charlie W. Starr, Winged Lion Press, 2012, pp. 6–9.

———. *The Lion, the Witch and the Wardrobe*. HarperCollins, 1950.

———. *The Magician's Nephew*. HarperCollins, 1955.

———. "The Man Born Blind." *The Dark Tower and Other Stories*, edited by Walter Hooper, Harcourt Brace, 1977, pp. 99–103.

———. "Meditation in a Toolshed." *Compelling Reason: Essays on Ethics and Theology*, edited by Walter Hooper, Harper Collins, 1996, pp. 53–57.

———. *Mere Christianity*. Touchstone, 1980.

———. "Miracles." *The Grand Miracle and Other Selected Essays on Theology and Ethics from God in the Dock*, edited by Walter Hooper, Ballantine, 1970, pp. 1–13.

———. *Miracles: A Preliminary Study*. Touchstone, 1975.

———. "Myth Became Fact." *God in the Dock: Essays on Theology and Ethics*, edited by Walter Hooper, Eerdmans, 1970, pp. 63–67.

———. "On Stories." *Essays Presented to Charles Williams*, edited by C. S. Lewis, Eerdmans, 1968, pp. 90–105.

———. *Out of the Silent Planet*. Scribner, 2003.

———. *Perelandra*. Scribner, 2003.

———. *The Personal Heresy: A Controversy* (with E. M. W. Tillyard). Oxford UP, 1939.

———. *The Pilgrim's Regress: An Allegorical Apology for Christianity, Reason and Romanticism*. Eerdmans, 1995.

———. "The Poison of Subjectivism." *Essay Collection & Other Short Pieces*, edited by Lesley Walmsley, Harper Collins, 2000, pp. 657–68.

———. "Prayer Manuscript." Marion E. Wade Center CSL MS-155. Unpublished.

———. *The Problem of Pain*. Macmillan, 1940.

———. "Psycho-Analysis and Literary Criticism." *Selected Literary Essays*, edited by Walter Hooper, Cambridge UP, 1969, pp. 286–300.

———. *Reflections on the Psalms*. Fontana, 1958.

———. "Religion: Reality or Substitute?" *Christian Reflections*, edited by Walter Hooper, Eerdmans, 1967, pp. 37–43.

———. *The Screwtape Letters with Screwtape Proposes a Toast*. HarperCollins, 1996.

———. *The Silver Chair*. HarperCollins, 1953.

———. "Sometimes Fairy Stories May Say Best What's to Be Said." *Of Other Worlds: Essays & Stories*, edited by Walter Hooper, Harvest/HBJ, 1966, pp. 35–38.

———. *Surprised by Joy: The Shape of My Early Life*. Harvest/ HBJ, 1955.

———. *They Stand Together: The Letters of C. S. Lewis to Arthur Greeves (1914–1963)*. Edited by Walter Hooper, Macmillan, 1979.

———. *That Hideous Strength*. Scribner, 2003.

———. *Till We Have Faces: A Myth Retold*. Harcourt Brace, 1985.

———. *Transposition and Other Addresses*. Geoffrey Bles, 1949.

———. "Transposition." *Transposition and Other Addresses*. Geoffrey Bles, 1949, pp. 9–20.

———. *The Voyage of the Dawn Treader*. HarperCollins, 1952.

———. "The Weight of Glory." Lewis, *The Weight of Glory*, pp. 3–19.

Works by Others

Como, James T. "Introduction." *At the Breakfast Table and Other Reminiscences*, edited by James T. Como, Macmillan, 1979, pp. xxi–xxxiv.

Edwards, Michael. "C. S. Lewis: Imagining Heaven." *Journal of Literature and Theology*, vol. 6, no. 2, June 1992, pp. 107–24.

Field of Dreams. Directed by Phil Alden Robinson, Universal, 1989.

Holy Bible. New International Version.

Hooper, Walter, "Preface." *Spirits in Bondage: A Cycle of Lyrics*. By C. S. Lewis, HBJ, 1984, pp. xi–xl.

Payne, Leanne. *Real Presence: The Holy Spirit in the Works of C. S. Lewis*. Cornerstone, 1979.

Works Briefly Referenced or Suggested for Additional Reading, Viewing, or Listening (in accessible contemporary editions)

Abbott, Edwin A. *Flatland: A Romance of Many Dimensions*. Warbler Classics, 2019.

Apuleius. *The Golden Ass*. Translated by Jack Lindsay, Indiana UP, 1962.

Aquinas, Thomas. *Summa Theologica. A Shorter Summa: The Essential Philosophical Passages of Saint Thomas Aquinas' Summa Theologica*. Edited by Peter Kreeft, Ignatius, 1993.

Athanasius. *De Incarnatione*. Translated by A. Robertson, Franklin Classics, 2018.

Barfield, Owen. *Poetic Diction: A Study in Meaning*. Barfield, 2014.

———. *Saving the Appearances: A Study in Idolatry*. Wesleyan UP, 1988.

———. *What Coleridge Thought*. Barfield, 2014.

Brown, Devin. *A Life Observed: A Spiritual Biography of C. S. Lewis*. Brazos, 2013.

Bultmann, Rudolff. *New Testament Mythology and Other Basic Writings*. Translated by Schubert M. Ogden, Fortress, 1984.

Coleridge, Samuel Taylor. *Biographia Literaria*. Literature Heritage Series, 2022.

Cowan, Donald. *Unbinding Prometheus: Education for the Coming Age*. Dallas Institute Publications, 1988.

Dante Alighieri. *The Divine Comedy*. Translated by Dorothy Sayers, Penguin, 1986. 3 vols.

Duriez, Colin. *C. S. Lewis: A Biography of Friendship*. Wilkinson House, 2013.

Edwards, Bruce. *A Rhetoric of Reading: C. S. Lewis's Defense of Western Literacy*. BYU, 1986.

Frazer, Sir James George. *The Golden Bough*. Digireads.com Publishing, 2019.

Guite, Malcolm. *Faith, Hope and Poetry: Theology and the Poetic Imagination*. Ashgate, 2012.

Honda, Mineko. *The Imaginative World of C. S. Lewis: A Way to Participate in Reality*. UP of America, 2000.

Interstellar. Directed by Christopher Nolan, Warner Brothers, 2014.

Kierkegaard, Soren. *Concluding Unscientific Postscript*. Edited by Alastair Hannay, Cambridge UP, 2009.

The Matrix. Directed by The Wachowski Brothers, Warner Brothers, 1999.

MacDonald, George. *Unspoken Sermons: Series I, II, III Complete and Unabridged*. Classics Reprint Series, 2016.

Otto, Rudolf. *The Idea of the Holy: An Inquiry into the Non-rational Factor in the Idea of the Divine and Its Relation to the Rational*. Translated by John W. Harvey, Pantianos Classics, 1923.

Pascal, Blaise. *Pensees*. Introduction by T. S. Eliot, Dover Thrift Edition, 2018.

Plato. *The Republic*. Translated by Allan Bloom, Basic Books, 2016.

Root, Jerry. Splendour in the Dark. Intervarsity, 2020.

Rush. *2112*. Produced by Terry Brown, Anthem Records, 1976.

Ruskin, John. *Selected Writings*. Edited by Dinah Birch, Oxford UP, 2009.

Sayer, George. *Jack: A Life of C. S. Lewis*. Crossway, 1988.

Schakel, Peter. *Imagination and the Arts in C. S. Lewis: Journeying to Narnia and Other Worlds*. U of Missouri P, 2002.

Schakel, Peter, and Charles A. Huttar. *Word and Story in C. S. Lewis: Language and Narrative in Theory and Practice*. Wipf & Stock, 1991.

Sophocles. *Oedipus the King. The Three Theban Plays.* Translated by Robert Fagles, Penguin, 1984.

Spenser, Edmund. *The Fairie Queene.* Penguin, 1979.

Star Wars. Directed by George Lucas, 20th Century Fox, 1977.

Starr, Charlie W. *The Faun's Bookshelf: C. S. Lewis on Why Myth Matters.* Kent State UP, 2018.

———. *Light: C. S. Lewis's First and Final Short Story.* Winged Lion Press, 2012.

Theologia Germanica. Just and Sinner, 2020.

Tolkien, J. R. R. *The Annotated Hobbit.* Edited by Douglas A. Anderson, Houghton Mifflin, 2002.

———. "Mythopoeia." *Tree and Leaf,* Harper Collins, 2001, pp. 85–90.

Ward, Michael. *After Humanity: A Guide to C. S. Lewis's* The Abolition of Man. Word on Fire, 2021.

Williams, Charles. *The Place of the Lion.* Bibliotech Press, 2012.

Index